9/18/09

Brian + Jen,

I wish you many years of happiness, love + laughter. Your honeymoon will go by so fast, so here is something to help bring you back to Spain!

Love Always,

Brian

COOK ESPAÑA, DRINK ESPAÑA!

A CULINARY JOURNEY AROUND THE FOOD AND DRINK OF SPAIN

COOK ESPAÑA,

A CULINARY JOURNEY AROUND THE FOOD AND DRINK OF SPAIN

DRINK ESPAÑA!

JOHN RADFORD & MARIO SANDOVAL

PHOTOGRAPHY BY JEAN-BLAISE HALL

MITCHELL BEAZLEY

Cook España, Drink España!
by John Radford and Mario Sandoval

First published in Great Britain in 2007 by Mitchell Beazley,
an imprint of Octopus Publishing Group Limited,
2–4 Heron Quays, London E14 4JP.
An Hachette Livre UK Company
www.hachettelivre.co.uk
www.octopusbooks.co.uk

This edition published 2009
Distributed in the U.S. and Canada by Octopus Books USA:
c/o Hachette Book Group USA
237 Park Avenue
New York NY 10017

The publishers will be grateful for any information that will assist them in keeping future editions up to date. Although all reasonable care has been taken in the preparation of this book, neither the publishers nor the authors can accept any liability for any consequence arising from the use thereof, or the information contained therein.

The authors have asserted their moral rights.

ISBN-13: 978 1 84533 459 8

A CIP catalog record for this book is available from the Library of Congress.

Set in Absara, Frutiger, and Goudy

Color reproduction by United Graphics in Singapore
Printed and bound by Toppan in China

NOTES
This book contains dishes made with raw or lightly-cooked eggs and meat. It is prudent for vulnerable people, such as pregnant and nursing mothers, invalids, the elderly, babies, and young children, to avoid uncooked or lightly-cooked dishes made with eggs and meat.

Meat and poultry should be cooked thoroughly. To test if poultry is cooked, pierce the flesh through the thickest part with a skewer or fork—the juices should run clear, never pink or red.

Commissioning Editor: Rebecca Spry
Senior Editor: Leanne Bryan
Executive Art Editor: Nicky Collings
Designer: Lizzie Ballantyne
Photographer: Jean-Blaise Hall
Production Controller: Lucy Carter

Introduction	6
Andalucía	10
Aragón	22
Asturias	32
Baleares	42
Canarias	52
Cantabria	62
Castilla y León	72
Castilla-La Mancha	84
Cataluña	96
Extremadura	108
Galicia	118
La Rioja	128
Madrid	140
Murcia	150
Navarra	160
País Vasco	170
Valencia	180
Recommended restaurants	190
Index	192

Since the new constitution of 1978, Spain as a country has returned to the regional cultural diversity it enjoyed in the past, and those of us who have never ventured beyond the Costas may not yet have realized just what this diversity is all about. Nowhere is this more apparent than in gastronomy: Spain's food, wine, and other drinks such as *sidra* (cider) and *pacharán* have a strong local cultural heritage, and modern restaurant techniques are bringing classic dishes into the 21st century, just as modern winemaking methods are reinventing the classic Spanish wine areas.

This book is a celebration of the diversity of Spanish culture as seen through its food and drink and its mealtime traditions, always based on the family model and revolving around the *comida*, the most important meal of the day, traditionally eaten at about 2 p.m. after copious tapas and before the siesta. *Comida* simply means "meal," which shows the importance

Introduction

attached to it. The tradition dates back to the time when schools and businesses started work very early in the morning in the summer and the working day was over by early afternoon, so the family could come together for a meal, before sleeping through the afternoon heat.

The full "menu" for the Spanish gastronomic day starts with *desayuno* (breakfast), traditionally accompanied by a *café con leche* (milky coffee) and a brandy, which may be mixed together to become a *carajillo*—this is known colloquially as *hacer las camas*: "to make the beds." A midmorning bite is *almuerzo*, which is generally translated as "lunch" although "snack" might be more accurate.

For those hardy enough to survive the rigors of the *comida* at 2 p.m., there's always the *merienda*, which roughly equates to afternoon tea, and might be served around 6 p.m.—another light meal to keep you going until dinnertime. In Spain they eat late—seldom before 9 p.m. and often after 10 p.m., and this is *cena*, which translates as "dinner" but is probably better described as "supper." Although it's a full meal it's usually much lighter than the *comida*. In the days when most Spaniards toiled in the fields all day and every day, some healthy appetites were generated.

In the 21st century this has translated into a wonderful panoply of regional foods, most of them based on the raw materials that were available locally in the days before refrigerated trucks could whisk Galician shellfish to Madrid restaurants overnight. Many of the most popular and intriguing recipes stem from the days when poor families had to be inventive with what few ingredients they could afford. *Migas* from Aragon and Navarra is a good example—

a dish of dry bread crumbs with whatever was left over from the last meal, perhaps a bit of *chorizo*, ham, cheese, even fruit in some cases, and it's absolutely delicious. Another Spanish staple, *menestra*, is a vegetable stew made with whatever happens to be in season, and is also a relic of these times. The name derives from the Spanish word *menester*, which means "want" or "need," illustrating its origins perfectly. Today it's more popular than ever, and rightly so.

There is a saying that "God created Spain to show the rest of Europe that there is an alternative." It's certainly true in the kitchen.

ABOUT THE AUTHORS

Mario Sandoval is a phenomenon amongst chefs in Spain. In 2004 he won the national Cooks' Championship and his first Michelin star at the age of 27—the youngest chef in Spain ever to do so. He is the son and grandson of chefs at the family restaurant Coque at Humanes de Madrid, 18 miles southwest of Madrid, just off the A42 Madrid–Toledo *Autopista*. He studied in Madrid and Barcelona before taking to the range, and has revolutionized the style and appeal of the restaurant. He represented Spain at the Bocuse d'Or festival in Lyon, and has won many other accolades in his native Madrid, in Spain nationally and beyond. His food style is very much "modern Spanish"—creating new tastes, styles, and recipes that take the best of Spanish regional cookery and reinvent them for the 21st century.

John Radford joined the wine trade in 1972, started lecturing on wine in 1975 and writing about it in 1977. He continued wine-trade consultancy until 1986, after which he went into journalism full time, including radio and television training and, from 1993, BBC radio, first with BBC East and latterly with BBC South-East in Sussex. He now presents a weekly program on local commercial radio in West Sussex. He writes or has written for most of the food and wine magazines including *Wine International*, *Decanter*, *Harpers Wine and Spirit Weekly*, *BBC Good Food*, and many others. His book, *The New Spain* (Mitchell Beazley), won four international awards in 1999. In addition he cowrote the *Mitchell Beazley Guide to Sweet and Fortified Wines* in 2000 and published *The Wines of Rioja* in 2004 ("Best European Wine Book" at the Livre Gourmand Awards in Versailles, 2005), as well as contributing chapters on Spain and Spanish wine to several guide-books and encyclopedias including the award-winning annual *Wine Report*. In 2005 he was awarded the *Premio Especial de Comunicación, Mejor Labor Informativa Continuada Relacionada Alimentos de España* by the Ministry of Agriculture in Madrid, reflecting his ongoing work on Spanish wines.

Abbreviations used in the text:

WINES

DO—*Denominación de Origen*: the main appellation for quality wines in Spain. It guarantees the origin and that certain quality-control checks have been applied

DOCa—*Denominación de Origen Calificada*: a "higher" appellation for wines of higher quality (there are two—Rioja and Priorat)

DOQ—*Denominació d'Origen Qualificada* (as above but in the Catalan language)

DO de Pago—individual estates (*pagos*) with international acclaim

VCPRD—*Vinos de Calidad Producido en Regiones Determinadas*: a "junior" version of the DO for wine areas on the way up

VdlT—*Vinos de la Tierra*: country wines

FOOD

The *Denominación de Origen* (DO, as above) is awarded to local produce and ingredients—e.g. ham, cheeses, fruit, olive oil, and charcuterie—which have shown consistent excellence over a long period of time. Other regional foods may be styled *Denominación Específica* (DE) or *Indicación Geográfica Protegida* (IGP), which protect the name from use by other regions of Spain.

NAMES AND SPELLINGS

Bodega—a wine producer or wine merchant, or the wine-cellar in a restaurant. Usually in the plural when used as a company name e.g. Bodegas Berberana

Adega—as above but in Galego (Galicia)

Celler—as above but in Catalan (Catalonia)

Cava—as above (Catalonia)

Crianza—wine that has been aged for at least two years, with six months or more in oak

Reserva—wine that has been aged for at least three years, with 12 months or more in oak

Gran Reserva—wine that has been aged for at least five years, with 18 months or more in oak

Unusual equipment and methods:

sifón iSi—a culinary-standard cream-whipping syphon fitted with a nitrous oxide gas cylinder

Roner digital thermostat—a thermostat with a precision temperature control. Useful for sous-vide cooking

sous-vide—the practice of slow-cooking food at precise, low temperatures in vacuum-packed plastic sealable bags. The term is French for 'vacuum-packed'

Thermomix—a food processor that also weighs, cooks, chops, crushes, emulsifies, whips, mixes, steams, blends, kneads, grinds, simmers, grates, and mills

Andalucía (Andalusia), Spain's second-largest region, played a seminal part in the origins of wine in western Europe. The city of Cádiz was founded in 1100 B.C. by Phoenician traders, and colonized around 500 B.C. by Greeks from the eastern Mediterranean, who brought their families, livestock, and, most importantly, vines with them. Three hundred years later, the Romans arrived and organized vine-growing and winemaking around modern-day Jerez.

Andalucía's eight provinces include Almería; Granada, the Moorish capital for seven centuries and home of the magnificent Alhambra palace; Málaga; Córdoba, with its magnificent mosque; Jaén; Huelva; and Cádiz, famous for the 1587 raid in which Sir Francis Drake's fleet destroyed the Spanish navy in the harbor. The westernmost province is Sevilla (Seville), the regional capital.

Andalucía specialties are numerous. The region is the virgin olive oil capital of Spain, with 15 established or transitional *denominaciones de origen* (DOs; *see* page 9). There's also a region-wide DO for mackerel and frigate mackerel, which are caught from Almería to Huelva.

Andalucía

Classic cured hams come from Córdoba, Granada, and Sierra de Huelva. The last includes the world-famous *jamón de bellota*, from free-range, acorn-fed pigs. *Queso serranía de Ronda* is a goats cheese made in the highlands of the province of Málaga.

Andalucía doesn't stint on vegetables, either. *Espárrago de Huétor-Tájar* is the asparagus grown in the cool mountains of Granada, and the *tomate de la Cañada-Níjar* of Granada (although technically a fruit) is also included in the list of regional specialties.

In recent years, the wine vinegar produced in Cádiz, Córdoba, and Huelva has come to prominence, as TV chefs have discovered the delights of Sherry vinegar in particular.

The most recent fruit DO awarded in the region is *Pasas de Málaga*, which governs the production of giant, juicy Muscatel raisins. *Chirimoya de la Costa Tropical Granada-Málaga* is the DO for custard-apples grown in Granada and Málaga, and the *Cítricos de Huelva* DO covers all manner of citrus fruit, including oranges, grapefruit, mandarins, clemetines, and lemons.

In terms of sweet things, *miel de Granada*, honey of Granada, has its own DO, while *alfajor de Medina Sidonia* (Sevilla) is a nougat made with honey, almonds, cinnamon, and other spices. Finally, Sevilla also offers *mantecada de Estepa*, a traditional Christmas pastry.

This popular dish is Córdoba's take on *gazpacho*, the world-famous chilled tomato soup from southern Spain. Classically, *salmorejo* is made in a mortar or *dornillo* (wooden bowl). Traditionalists insist that the texture is more authentic when it's made by hand, but using a food processor is much quicker. Although this refreshing soup is usually served chilled, it's also delicious when eaten hot in cold weather.

Salmorejo Cordobés

Chilled tomato soup with chopped egg and ham

INGREDIENTS (SERVES 4)

1lb 12oz very ripe tomatoes

2 garlic cloves, peeled

7oz day-old bread, crusts removed, cut into cubes

½ cup olive oil

1 tablespoon Sherry wine vinegar

salt and freshly ground black pepper, to taste

GARNISH

2 eggs

1 teaspoon wine vinegar

1 tablespoon olive oil

2oz Iberian ham or *serrano* ham, thinly sliced and finely shredded

4 slices of thin, crisp toast (optional)

To make the soup, remove any stalks and wash the tomatoes. Chop roughly in a food processor. Then add the garlic and blend again to form a thin tomato puree. Strain through a sieve into a large bowl, and discard the seeds and skin.

Stir the bread into the tomato puree. Set aside to soak for four to 12 hours in the refrigerator. Then pour the tomato and bread mixture into a food processor and blend to a velvety smooth soup with a creamy consistency. Keep the food processor running while slowly drizzling in the olive oil, then the vinegar, a pinch of salt, and some black pepper. If necessary, thin the consistency with a few tablespoons of cold water. Pour the *salmorejo* into a bowl and put in the refrigerator to chill.

For the garnish, put the eggs in a saucepan, cover with cold water, and add a pinch of salt and a teaspoonful of vinegar. Bring to a boil and cook for 10 minutes. Carefully transfer the eggs to a bowl of ice water to cool quickly. When cold enough to handle, peel off the shells under running water. Part the whites from the yolks before finely chopping both separately.

Ladle a portion of the *salmorejo* into each bowl. Drizzle a few drops of olive oil over the soup. Garnish with a little chopped egg yolk and egg white, strips of ham, and a slice of thin, crisp toast, if desired.

WINE TIPS

SPECIAL OCCASION: **Lustau Single Cask Amontillado, Jerez (€€€)**
SUNDAY LUNCH: **Fernando de Castilla Amontillado, Jerez (€€)**
EVERYDAY: **Viña AB, González Byass, Jerez (€)**

The notorious heat of Andalucía influences many of its traditional dishes. Without doubt, the best known are the tasty chilled soups that make good use of locally grown ingredients, such as almonds and tomatoes. This delicious almond soup reflects the Arab heritage of the region. The provinces of Sevilla and Málaga both claim to have invented it, although similar versions are served all over southern Spain.

Ajo blanco Malagueño

Chilled white almond soup, Málaga-style

INGREDIENTS (SERVES 4)

2 garlic cloves, peeled

1 cup blanched almonds,
   roughly chopped

salt, to taste

1 tablespoon Sherry wine vinegar

3 tablespoons olive oil

3oz day-old white bread, crusts
   removed, cut into cubes

2 cups water

GARNISH

olive oil

1/2 cup white grapes

slices of melon

Crush the garlic, almonds, and a little salt together in a mortar and pestle to form a smooth paste. Then slowly stir in the vinegar, followed by the olive oil, mixing well. Set aside to chill in the refrigerator overnight to thicken.

Next day, put the bread in a bowl and cover with the water. Allow to soak for 5 minutes, or until softened. Transfer the soggy bread to a food processor. Pour in the almond paste and blend together at high speed, adding any water remaining in the bowl to make a smooth, creamy soup.

Serve the soup in bowls, garnished with a drizzle of olive oil, a few grapes, and slices of melon. You could use other combinations of fruit or nuts as a garnish, depending on what you have in the refrigerator.

WINE TIPS

SPECIAL OCCASION: **Amontillado del Duque, González Byass, Jerez (€€€€)**
SUNDAY LUNCH: **Pastrana Manzanilla Pasada, Hidalgo, Jerez (€€)**
EVERYDAY: **Tío Pepe, González Byass, Jerez (€)**

In Andalucía, no part of a pig is wasted. Some of the less familiar and cheaper cuts of pork are used to create dishes with outstanding and memorable flavors. The stars of this recipe are the *pluma*, from the front of the loin, the *secreto* from the side bacon, and the *sorpresa*, from the fore shoulder. Their succulent meat marries perfectly with the sweet wine sauce.

Manjar de Ibéricos en diferentes texturas
Iberian charcuterie casserole with a sweet wine sauce

INGREDIENTS (SERVES 4)
1lb *secreto*

1lb 10oz *sorpresa*

2 1/2 tablespoons cooking salt

2 onions, finely chopped

6 carrots, finely chopped

4 leeks, finely chopped

salt and pepper, to taste

4 peaches, skinned and sliced

1 1/4 cups Montilla or Sherry
   Pedro Ximénez

2/3 cup water

GARNISH
7oz morels (mushrooms), blanched
   in boiling water

fresh rosemary or thyme
   (optional)

Wash and trim the *secreto*, and *sorpresa*, and keep the trimmings. Rub the salt all over the *secreto* and leave for 1 1/2 hours. Then wash away the salt under cold running water and dry well. Cut the *secreto* into 1/2 inch-thick slices. Layer the slices into a 2lb loaf pan, lined with plastic wrap, vacuum-pack into a cooking bag, and cook in a *sous-vide* water bath cooker at 160°F for at least 10 hours, or until cooked through. Then chill rapidly in the freezer and set aside.

Meanwhile, put the *sorpresa*, 1 of the onions, the carrots, leeks, and a pinch of salt into a pressure cooker and cover with cold water. Secure the lid, bring to a boil, and cook over a low heat for 25 minutes, or until the *sorpresa* is cooked through. Then remove the *sorpresa* and set aside.

Preheat the oven to 300°F. Put the pork trimmings and remaining chopped onion in a roasting pan and roast in the oven for 25 minutes until browned and cooked through. After about 20 minutes, add the peaches to the roasting pan. While still hot, transfer the contents of the roasting pan to a saucepan and pour over the wine and water. Bring to a boil and simmer until the liquid has reduced by half. Strain into a clean saucepan and continue boiling until the liquid has thickened to form a sauce.

To prepare the pork for serving, cut the *secreto* into cubes and brown under a low broiler and slice the *sorpresa*.

Put some *secreto* on each plate and glaze with a little wine sauce. Arrange a few slices of hot *sorpresa* on the side. Sprinkle a few grains of salt over the meat and garnish with a few morels, glazed with a spoonful of the wine sauce, and fresh rosemary or thyme, if desired.

WINE TIPS

SPECIAL OCCASION: **Ramos Paul, El Chantre, Sierras de Málaga (€€€)**
SUNDAY LUNCH: **Señorío de Nevada Syrah Merlot, Granada Sur-Ouest (€€)**
EVERYDAY: **Reserva Privada, Príncipe Alfonso, Sierras de Málaga (€)**

Those that associate the world of tapas with a wonderfully appetizing array of little dishes of food, which is typical of northern Spain, may be a bit taken aback when they walk into an Andaluz tapas bar for the first time and are confronted with an empty counter. This is because Andaluz tapas are always fried and need to be cooked to order just before serving.

Esturión adobado en gran fritura con mayonesa ligera de lima

Deep-fried sturgeon with lime mayonnaise

INGREDIENTS (SERVES 4)
2 garlic cloves, peeled
salt, to taste
1 teaspoon dried oregano
1 teaspoon cumin seeds
3 tablespoons Sherry wine vinegar
pinch of paprika
pinch of ground caraway seeds
2 teaspoons lemon juice
2lb 4oz fillet of sturgeon

FOR THE LIME MAYONNAISE
1 egg
salt, to taste
2 teaspoons lime juice
3/4 cup sunflower oil
2 tablespoons olive oil

FOR FRYING
2/3 cup besan (gram flour)
virgin olive oil

GARNISH
finely grated lime zest
fresh herbs (optional)

For a marinade, grind the garlic, a pinch of salt, oregano, and cumin seeds in a mortar and pestle to form a paste. Then stir in the vinegar, paprika, ground caraway seeds, and lemon juice. Cut the sturgeon fillet into 2 inch strips and coat in the marinade. Keep in the refrigerator for 24 hours.

For the mayonnaise, crack the egg into a bowl. Beat in a pinch of salt and the lime juice. Gradually beat in the oils, beating vigorously to form a smooth, glossy mayonnaise. Cover with waxed paper and set aside in the refrigerator.

Drain the marinade from the sturgeon and coat the pieces of fish in besan. Heat plenty of virgin olive oil to 350°F in a large saucepan and fry the fish, in batches, for about 8 minutes until crisp on the outside and juicy on the inside. Remove from the saucepan and put on a baking sheet lined with kitchen towel to drain off any excess oil.

Arrange 3 or 4 strips of sturgeon in the center of each plate with a few drops of lime mayonnaise. Garnish with shreds of finely grated lime zest and some fresh herbs, if desired.

WINE TIPS

SPECIAL OCCASION: **Sacristia Oloroso Seco, Sánchez Romate, Jerez (€€€)**
SUNDAY LUNCH: **Blanco de Blancas Nobles, Barranco Oscuro, Contraviesa-Alpujarra (€€)**
EVERYDAY: **Castillo de San Diego, Barbadillo, Cádiz (€)**

Wines of Andalucía

The most famous Andaluz wine is Sherry. Wine has been made in the region around Jerez certainly since about 500 B.C., and from the Middle Ages to the 19th century Sherry was widely considered to be the finest wine in the world, largely because, as a fortified wine, it could survive rough handling and primitive transport systems. Until 1933, wine made all over the region was shipped to Jerez and exported under the Sherry name, but in the 20th century, the various wines made outside the Jerez area were renamed according to their individual origins.

DO JEREZ/XÉRÈS/SHERRY Y MANZANILLA DE SANLÚCAR

That's the official full name of this, the Sherry DO, and wine using this *denominación* may be made from grapes (largely Palomino with some Pedro Ximénez (PX) and Moscatel) grown in and around the three towns of Jerez, El Puerto de Santa María, and Sanlúcar de Barrameda, in the province of Cádiz. It comes in a number of styles:

Fino is pale, bone-dry, and matures under a coating of natural yeast known as *flor*, which gives it a fresh, nutty flavor. It makes an excellent apéritif and is a classic partner for tapas and seafood. It also matches well with spicy oriental dishes. *Finos* made in the coolest area, around Sanlúcar, may be called **manzanilla**.

Amontillado is a *fino* that has been aged for a longer period, and has started to mellow and turn darker in the glass. Still completely dry in their natural state, these wines go well with meat and game. Most commercial *amontillado*, however, is blended with sweetening wines.

Oloroso is a wine that didn't grow a covering of yeast during its maturation period and tends to be a rich walnut-brown in color. Again, it's completely dry in its natural state, but is very often sweetened and sold as **Cream**.

PX and **Moscatel** are sweet wines made with the named grape: old PX may be almost completely black in color and is arguably the sweetest wine in the world.

Very old wines may be labeled with an average age: 12, 15, 20 (also VOS—Very Old Sherry) or 30 years (VORS—Very Old Rare Sherry).

DO MONTILLA-MORILES

This is an area in the province of Córdoba which makes traditional fortified wines in the style of Jerez, and with the same names: *fino*, *amontillado*, etc., but mainly with PX grapes. The style tends to be more robust than Sherry and there are two additional categories: **crianza** wines are unfortified but aged in cask or tank, and **jóvenes** (young wines) are young wines that are bottled straight after the vintage to retain their freshness.

DO MÁLAGA Y SIERRAS DE MÁLAGA

Traditionally, this area made big, sweet, fortified wines whose grapes had been sun-dried before pressing, but the compass is greater now. Unfortified red and white wines are made, typically in the highland areas where the nights are cooler. Sweet wines are labeled *Málaga*, and other wines *Sierras de Málaga*.

DO CONDADO DE HUELVA

In the 19th century this region made Sherry-type wines and sent them to Jerez, but today that is, of course, illegal. They still make fortified styles, almost universally from the Zalema grape. *Pálido* is pale and dry and *viejo* is an aged wine, usually sweetened. In addition there is also a light *joven* wine.

OTHER WINES

Andalucía has 16 Vino de la Tierra (VdlT) areas. Only the most prominent are listed below.

VdlT Cádiz This covers the entire province and allows mainly the Sherry companies to make light, unfortified white wines from the Palomino grape. In recent years, a wider range of grape varieties has been planted and some good wines are being made.

VdlT Contraviesa-Alpujarra This covers an area from the mountains to the coast in the province of Granada, growing a range of grapes. The highland vineyards (over 3,300 feet) make some excellent whites from Vigiriega and reds from Garnacha, as well as sparkling wines made from both red and white grapes.

VdlT Granada Sur-Ouest As its name implies, this is southwest of the city of Granada, and there are several small bodegas working hard to establish the area with wines made from Syrah, Merlot, and Cabernet Sauvignon grapes.

OTHER DRINKS

One of the great classics of Andalucía is Brandy de Jerez: brandy aged in old Sherry casks, often for many years. The base wine for the brandy is, typically, made from the Airén grape grown and distilled in Castilla-La Mancha, although a very few of the finest brandies are distilled from wine made from Palomino grapes grown in Jerez.

The first Brandy de Jerez to carry the name was Fundador by Pedro Domecq, which came onto the market in 1874 and is still a bestseller today. It used to be a tradition in Spain to take a small glass with a cup of coffee with breakfast, a practice known as *hacer las camas* ("to make the beds"—i.e. before going to work), or to mix the brandy with the coffee to make a *carajillo*. Because of its aging in old Sherry casks, even the cheaper Brandy de Jerez is usually very palatable, but the very best can hold up against any brandy in the world: elegant, mature, fragrant, and a perfect, lingering end to an excellent meal. Look for the words *Solera Gran Reserva* on the label, and names with which to conjure include Le Panto (González Byass), Carlos Primero (Pedro Domecq), Conde de Osborne, Cardenal Mendoza (Sánchez Romate), Gran Duque de Alba (Williams & Humbert), and Rey Fernando de Castilla. These are truly sublime.

Main Bodegas
(listed in alphabetical order), PRODUCER NAME; town/village; web/E-mail address; best wines (f = fortified, u = unfortified)
A star (*) indicates particularly good quality.

DO JEREZ/XERES/SHERRY Y MANZANILLA DE SANLUCAR
www.sherry.org

EMILIO LUSTAU; Jerez; www.emiliolustau.com; Solera range (f), Almacenista range (f)*

GONZALEZ BYASS; Jerez; www.gonzalezbyass.es; Tío Pepe (f), VOS/VORS range (f)*, Moncloa range (u)

HIDALGO-LA GITANA; Sanlúcar; www.lagitana.es; La Gitana (f), Pastrana (f)*, Napoleon range (f)

OSBORNE; El Puerto; www.osborne.es; Fino Quinta (f)*, VOS/VORS range (f)

PEDRO DOMECQ; Jerez; www.domecq.es; Fino la Ina (f)*; Amontillado 51-1ª (f)*, VORS range (f)*

RAINERA PEREZ MARIN; Sanlúcar; www.laguita.com; La Guita Manzanilla (f)*, Miraflores range (u)

REY FERNANDO DE CASTILLA; Jerez; www.fernandodecastilla.com; entire range (f)*

SANDEMAN; Jerez; www.sandeman.com; Royal range (f)*

TRADICION; Jerez; www.bodegastradicion.com; entire range (f)*

VALDESPINO; Jerez; www.grupoestevez.com; Inocente (f); Tio Mateo (f)

WILLIAMS & HUMBERT; Jerez; www.williams-humbert.com; Don Zoilo (f), Solera Especial range (f)*

DO MONTILLA-MORILES
www.montilla-moriles.org

ALVEAR; Montilla; www.alvear.es; Capataz (f), CB (f)*, Marques de Montilla (u)

PEREZ BARQUERO; Montilla; www.perezbarquero.com; Gran Barquero (f)

TORO ALBALA; Aguilar de la Frontera; www.talbala.com; Eléctrico range (f, u), Don PX (f)*

DO MÁLAGA Y SIERRAS DE MÁLAGA
www.vinomalaga.com

BENTOMIZ; Cómpeta; www.bodegasbentomiz.com; Ariyanas dulce (u)*

DESCALZOS VIEJOS; Ronda; paco@retamero-salesi.com; Descalzos Viejos (u)*

FRIEDRICH SCHATZ; Ronda; www.f-schatz.com; Finca Sanguijela (u)

LOPEZ HERMANOS; Málaga; www.lopezhermanos.com; entire range (f)*

LOS BUJEOS; Ronda; www.eljuncal.com; Pasos Largos (u)

PRINCIPE ALFONSO DE HOHENLOE; Ronda; www.haciendas-espana.com; Principe Alfonso (u)

TELMO RODRIGUEZ; Málaga; cia@fer.es; Molino Real (u)*

DO CONDADO DE HUELVA
www.vinoscondadohuelva.com

OLIVEROS; Bollullos par del Condado; www.bodegasoliveros.com; Viña Oliveros (u), Vino de Pasas (f)

PRIVILEGIO DEL CONDADO; Bollullos par del Condado; www.vinicoladelcondado.com; Prvilegio (u), Misterio (f)

VdlT DE CADIZ

See DO Jerez (above)

VdlT CONTRAVIESA-ALPUJARRA

BARRANCO OSCURO; Cádiar; www.barrancooscuro.com; Blancas Nobles (u)*, 1368 Barranco Oscuro (u)*

VdlT GRANADA SUR-OUEST

SEÑORÍO DE NEVADA; Villamena; bodegass_nevada@teleline.es; Señorío de Nevada

Aragón was one of the two independent kingdoms that laid the foundations of modern Spain. In 1469, the future King Ferdinand of Aragón married Queen Isabella of Castilla, which started the process of creating a united Spain. Today, Aragón is a region as famous for its winter sports in the Pyrenees as for its fresh produce and its wines, many of which represent astonishingly good value for money. The capital is the city of Zaragoza, which was founded by the Romans. The region consists of three provinces: Zaragoza, surrounding the capital; Teruel to the south; and Huesca to the north, which shares its northern border with France at the summit of the Pyrenees, including the highest point, Aneto Peak, at 11,168 feet.

Aragón

LOCAL SPECIALTIES

Jamón de Teruel is the cured ham of the region, made from a local breed of pig that is a Large White/Landrace/Duroc cross. *Ternasco de Aragón* is a local lamb highly admired for its meat and farmed all over the region. Meat products such as *longaniza* (spiced pork sausage), *lomo* (cured pork loin), *morcilla* (black pudding), and *chorizo* (spicy sausage) are produced throughout Aragón. More unusual products include *conserva de cerdo en aceite* (pork loin and rib preserved in olive oil), *cecina* (air-dried or smoked beef), and *ternasco ahumado* (smoked lamb). The *melocotón de Calanda* is a particularly sweet strain of peach grown in the northeast of the province of Teruel. Olives from Caspe in the province of Zaragoza are recognized as a crop in their own right, separate from the oil industry, although *aceite de bajo Aragón* (extra-virgin olive oil) is made in Zaragoza and Teruel; in addition, there's a generic quality mark for the whole region. This is also asparagus country, and the *espárragos de Navarra*, as its name implies, is shared with neighboring Navarra. The *cebolla dulce de Fuentes* (sweet onion) and the *borraja* (a relative of borage) grow only in the autumn here and in Navarra.

Aragón is one of Spain's leading cheese producers, with both *fresco* (fresh) and *curado* (cured, usually with olive oil) styles as well as *semicurado*. The milk of cows, sheep, and goats is used, with *artesanal* styles being the most favored. *Azafrán de Aragón* (saffron) is one of the most highly prized ingredients in all of Spain—and the most expensive, at approximately €1 ($1.5) per gram (0.04oz).

Shank of *ternasco* (young lamb) has been a favorite ingredient in this region for many centuries. The tenderness and flavor of the meat is exclusive to sheep reared in the locality. In this recipe, the contrast between the earthy taste of the mushrooms and the sweetness of the figs complements the meat beautifully. Just bear in mind that you may need to order the caul fat from your butcher in advance.

Jarrete de ternasco de Aragón con higos y setas
Tender Aragón lamb shank with figs and mushrooms

INGREDIENTS (SERVES 4)

4 lamb shanks
salt and pepper, to taste
1 tablespoon olive oil
2 red bell peppers, finely chopped
2 green bell peppers,
    finely chopped
3 onions, finely chopped
2 garlic cloves, finely chopped
3/4 cup white wine
3/4 cup red wine
2 cups beef stock
8 dried figs (stalks removed),
    chopped into small pieces
3/4 cup port
7oz button mushrooms, washed
    and sliced
2 tablespoons olive oil
sheet of caul fat, cut into 4 pieces
sprig of fresh marjoram,
    to garnish

Season the shanks with salt and pepper. Heat the olive oil in a flameproof casserole and brown the shanks all over. Remove the shanks from the casserole.

In the same oil, gently fry the peppers, onions, and garlic for about 15 minutes until softened. Return the shanks to the casserole and pour in the wine and stock. Bring to a boil and simmer until the lamb is tender when pricked with a skewer. Remove the shanks from the casserole and set aside. Strain the juices through a sieve. Set aside to use as the sauce for the dish.

Simmer the figs in the port for about 20 minutes. When the figs are soft and the port reduced, blend into a pulp.

Preheat the oven to 325°F. Spread the mushrooms on a baking sheet, drizzle over 1 tablespoon of olive oil and a sprinkling of salt. Roast in the oven for 25 minutes. Drain off any juices. Heat 1 tablespoon of olive oil in a skillet and sauté the mushrooms briefly until just browned.

Gently twist the bones out of the shanks, disturbing the meat as little as possible. Spread out the caul fat and use 1 sheet to wrap up each piece of meat, wrapping the fat several times around the meat to make it thicker, forming 4 neat cylinders. Stand the cylinders on a baking sheet and roast in the oven at 325°F for 3 minutes.

Place a spoonful of the fig pulp and sautéed mushrooms on each plate, and sit the shank beside. Glaze the top of the shank with a little sauce and drizzle a little more around the plate. Garnish with a sprig of fresh marjoram.

WINE TIPS

SPECIAL OCCASION: **Blecua, Viñas del Vero, Somontano (€€€)**
SUNDAY LUNCH: **Fagús Coto de Hayas, Aragonesas, Calatayud (€€)**
EVERYDAY: **Imperial Carinus Reserva, San Valero, Cariñena (€)**

Aragón is a fertile region, blessed with many rivers, and famous for growing magnificent vegetables. The markets are stacked with onions from Fuentes de Ebro, beet from Jalón, garlic from Bardallur, and cardoons (artichoke thistles) from Muel and Mozota. The mildness of *borrajas*, a green leafy vegetable first introduced to Spain from Africa by the Arabs, suits the mix of earthy and salty flavors in this soup perfectly.

Tallos de borrajas con arroz y almejas

Borrajas stems with rice and clams

INGREDIENTS (SERVES 4)

10oz *borrajas* stems (a green leaf with long white stems, similar to Swiss chard)

2 tablespoons olive oil

4 garlic cloves, peeled and chopped

1 tablespoon flour

4 cups fish stock

1 tablespoon chopped fresh parsley

3 tablespoons rice

9oz fresh clams (shells on)

salt and freshly ground black pepper, to taste

Wash the *borrajas* and shred the leaves. Heat the olive oil in a large saucepan and fry the garlic until golden. Then sprinkle in the flour and mix into the olive oil with a wooden spoon. Cook for 2 minutes over a moderate heat.

Add the fish stock, stirring continuously with a whisk, so that lumps do not form, then add the chopped parsley. When the stock starts to boil, add the *borrajas* and rice. Boil over a high heat for 15 minutes.

Then tip in the clams, cover the saucepan, and continue boiling for 3–4 minutes until the shells open. Turn off the heat, add a pinch of salt and a few twists of pepper, and stir well.

Ladle some of the *borrajas* and rice soup into each bowl. Garnish with the clams.

WINE TIPS

SPECIAL OCCASION: **Reyes de Aragón Ecológico Blanco, Calatayud (€€€)**
SUNDAY LUNCH: **Viñas del Vero Clarión Blanco, Somontano (€€)**
EVERYDAY: **Care Blanco Chardonnay, Bodegas Añadas, Cariñena (€)**

Poultry is a great specialty of Aragón, and this chicken stew is among the region's best-loved dishes. From village to village, it appears in many guises, but it's always the superb flavor of the rich red pepper, tomato, and onion sauce that lingers in the memory. Such tasty juices are just perfect for mopping up with lots of crusty bread.

Pollo al Chilindrón

Chicken stew, Chilindrón-style

INGREDIENTS (SERVES 4)

3 tablespoons olive oil

4 red bell peppers, washed
   and dried

1 large chicken, washed and
   jointed into 2 breasts and
   2 legs

salt and freshly ground black
   pepper, to taste

3 garlic cloves, chopped

2 onions, finely chopped

6oz piece of Iberian ham, or
   serrano ham, diced

14oz can chopped tomatoes

scallions, finely sliced, to garnish

Preheat the oven to 350°F. Rub 1 tablespoon of olive oil over the peppers. Put on a baking sheet and roast in the oven for 15 minutes. Set aside to cool, then peel and cut into ½ inch strips.

Season the chicken pieces with salt and pepper. Heat the remaining 2 tablespoons of olive oil in a flameproof casserole over a medium heat. Add the chicken and brown on all sides, then remove from the casserole and set aside.

In the same casserole, lightly fry the garlic, onions, and ham. When lightly browned, add the tomatoes and strips of pepper, and return the chicken pieces to the pot. Stir everything together well. Bring to a boil over a medium heat and simmer over a low heat for about 40 minutes, stirring from time to time, until the chicken is tender and cooked through. Adjust the seasoning if necessary.

Spoon a generous quantity of the red pepper and tomato sauce onto the center of each plate. Lay a chicken piece on top, slightly to one side. Garnish with a sprinkling of scallions.

WINE TIPS

SPECIAL OCCASION: **Marboré, Pirineos, Somontano (€€€)**
SUNDAY LUNCH: **Tres Picos, Borsao, Campo de Borja (€€)**
EVERYDAY: **Baltasar Gracián Garnacha Viñas Viejas, San Alejandro, Calatayud (€)**

The fruit that grows in Aragón is the inspiration for numerous delicious desserts. This recipe showcases the versatility of just one fruit: the apple. By using different varieties of apple and a range of cooking techniques, a refreshing dish of creamy and melting textures with sweet and sour flavors is created to delight the taste buds.

Bomba de manzana con crema ahumada de manzana caramelizada y gelatina de sidra

Apple cream bun with apple sorbet and cider gelatin dessert

INGREDIENTS (SERVES 4)

FOR THE CIDER GELATIN DESSERT
2 cups hard cider
3 sheets of leaf gelatin, soaked

FOR THE APPLE SORBET
3 cups water
1½ cup brown sugar
6 Granny Smith apples, peeled,
   quartered, and cored

FOR THE APPLE BUN
1lb 2oz cooking apples
3 tablespoons sugar
5 tablespoons butter
1 cup hard cider
6 sheets of leaf gelatin, soaked
1½ cups heavy cream

FOR THE LIGHT SYRUP
1½ cups water
⅔ cup brown sugar

For the cider gelatin dessert, heat the cider gently in a saucepan. When hot but not boiling, stir in the gelatin. Continue heating and stirring gently until the sheets have dissolved. Pour into a shallow dish. Allow to cool before putting in the refrigerator to set overnight. Before serving, cut into small cubes and keep in the refrigerator.

For the apple sorbet, heat the water and sugar gently in a saucepan. Boil the syrup until it becomes a light brown colour, then allow to cool. Blend the apples with the syrup to a smooth puree in a food processor. Pour into a plastic container and put in the freezer overnight until frozen.

For the apple buns, roast the apples with a little sugar and butter at 350°F for 20 minutes. Halfway through the cooking time, pour in the cider. When the apples are cooked, spoon the pulp and remaining cider into a large bowl, and discard the skin, core, and seeds. Add the gelatin and stir until the sheets have dissolved. Allow to cool.

Whip the cream, and fold it into the cooled apple mixture. Pour the apple cream into a plastic container, cover, and allow to set overnight in the refrigerator.

For the light syrup, heat the water and sugar gently in a saucepan. Boil the syrup until it becomes a light brown color, then allow to cool.

Drizzle a trail of light syrup across the middle of each plate. Use an ice-cream scoop to shape a ball from the apple cream. Place this apple "bun" on one side of the syrup line. Put a scoop of apple sorbet on the other side, and arrange a pile of cider gelatin cubes in between.

WINE TIPS

SPECIAL OCCASION: **Gewurztraminer, Enate, Somontano (€€€)**
SUNDAY LUNCH: **Coto de Hayas Moscatel, Aragonesas, Campo de Borja (€€)**
EVERYDAY: **Moscatel Ainzón, Santo Cristo, Campo de Borja (€)**

Wines of Aragón

Aragón has four DO wine areas, three in Zaragoza province and the fourth high in the Pyrenees in the province of Huesca. The last makes wines from mainly international varieties such as Cabernet Sauvignon and Merlot, although Tempranillo is widespread throughout the region. The three Zaragozano DOs—Calatayud, Campo de Borja, and Cariñena—languished in terms of exports until discovering that their ancient plantations of Garnacha and Cariñena could produce wonderful quality wines if the local cooperatives harvested at lower yields. Eventually, some co-ops merged and became limited companies, which allowed them to offer better prices for grapes from older vineyards. Many growers discovered they could produce half as much and get more money for their production. These are now some of the best-value wines in Spain. Sparkling wines are also made under the Cava DO; *see* Cataluña, page 105.

DO CALATAYUD

DO Calatayud is the southernmost of the Aragonés wine areas, based around the town of the same name. It was the first to exploit low-yielding old vines and to amalgamate old cooperatives into dynamic new companies.

DO CAMPO DE BORJA

DO Campo de Borja is a continuation southward of the Navarra DO into a more arid area but still well supplied with plantations of old vines.

DO CARINENA

DO Cariñena is almost as big as all other Aragonés wine areas put together. Its wines offer consistently good value for money at the budget end of the market.

DO SOMONTANO

DO Somontano is the most recent wine area in Aragón, high in the Pyrenees. The winemaking style here is completely different from the rest of Aragón, centered around international varieties, as well as Tempranillo and Garnacha.

OTHER WINES

VdlT Bajo Aragón Teruel (mainly) and Zaragoza: an improving area with some encouraging new investment.

The best wines are red and mainly Garnacha, with some Tempranillo, Cabernet Sauvignon, and Syrah.

VdlT Ribera del Queiles Zaragoza: a new venture. Only one notable bodega makes wine both here and across the border to the east in Navarra (*see* Navarra, page 168).

VdlT Valle del Cinca Huesca: another new venture driven by a major wine company—Codorníu from Cava country in the Cinca river valley.

Other wines of mainly local interest, although with the odd rising star, are made in the **VdlTs Valdejalón** (Zaragoza), **Campo de Belchite** (Zaragoza and Teruel), **Muniesa** (Teruel), **Ribera del Gállego-Cinco Villas** (Zaragoza), and **Tierra Baja de Aragón** (Zaragoza).

OTHER DRINKS

The small village of Colungo in Huesca (pop. 179) is a distillation center for spirits made from leftover grape pomace (www.aguardientescolungo.com). The basic spirit is *orujo* (as in Galicia), available as "natural" and oak-aged in barrel. It's also made with herbs, coffee, tea, fruit, flowers, and anise, in the style of *Patxaran* (*see* Navarra, page 169).

Main Bodegas

(listed in alphabetical order), PRODUCER NAME; town/village; web/E-mail address; best wines (r = red, w = white, p = pink) A star (*) indicates particularly good quality.

DO CALATAYUD
www.docalatayud.com.

JALON; Calatayud; www.castillodemaluenda.com; Castillo de Maluenda (r), Claraval (r)*

LANGA; Calatayud; www.bodegas-langa.com; Reyes de Aragón (r)

SAN ALEJANDRO; Miedes; www.san-alejandro.com; Viñas de Miedes (r), Baltasar Gracián (r)*

SAN GREGORIO; Cervera de la Cañada; www.bodegasangregorio.com; Monte Armantes (r)

DO CAMPO DE BORJA
www.campodeborja.com

ALTO MONCAYO; Bulbuente; www.bodegasaltomoncayo.com; Alto Moncayo (r), Aquilón (r)*

ARAGONESAS; Fuendejalón; www.bodegasaragonesas.com; Coto de Hayas (r), Fagús (r)*

BORDEJE; Ainzón; www.bodegasbordeje.com; Don Pablo (r), Pago de Romeroso (r)

BORSAO; Borja; www.bodegasborsao.com; Borsao (r), Tres Picos (r)*

SANTO CRISTO; Ainzón; www.bodegas-santo-cristo.com; Peñazuela (r), Viña Ainzón Reserva (r)

DO CARINENA
www.docarinena.com

ANADAS; Cariñena; www.carewines.com; Care (r, w)*

GRANDES VINOS; Cariñena; www.grandesvinos.com; Monasterio de las Viñas (r), Corona de Aragón (r)

GRAN DUCAY; Cariñena; www.bodegasanvalero.com; Monte Ducay (r), Carinus (r)*

SEÑORÍO DE AYLES; Mezalocha; www.bodegasayles.com; Aylés (r)

SOLAR DE URBEZO; Cariñena; www.solardeurbezo.es; Urbezo (r)

VICTORIA; Cariñena; www.bodegasvictoria.com; Dominio de Longaz (r), Longus (r)*

DO SOMONTANO
www.somontano.com

ENATE; Salas Bajas; www.enate.es; Enate (r, w, p), Merlot-Merlot (r)*

IRIUS; Barbastro; www.bodegairius.com; Absum (r, w)

LALANNE; Barbastro; www.bodegaslalanne.com; Lalanne (r), Leonor (r), Laura (r)

OSCA; Ponzano; www.bodegasosca.com; Osca (r), L'Ainsa (r)

OTTO BESTUÉ; Enate; www.bodega-ottobestue.com; Bestué (r, p), Finca Santa Sabina (r)*

PIRINEOS; Barbastro; www.bodegapirineos.com; Montesierra (r, w, p), Pirineos (r, w, p)

VINAS DEL VERO; Barbastro; www.vinasdelvero.com; Viñas del Vero (r, w, p), Gran Vos (r)*, Blecua (r)*

VdlT BAJO ARAGON

DOMINIO MAESTRAZGO; Alcorisa; www.dominiomaestrazgo.com; Dominio Maestrazgo (r), Rex Deus (r)*

VdlT RIBERA DEL QUEILES

GUELBENZU; Vierlas; www.guelbenzu.com; Guelbenzu Vierlas (r)

VdlT VALLE DEL CINCA

NUVIANA; San Miguel-Belver de Cinca; www.nuviana.com; Nuviana (r)

A sturias is unique in Spain in being a *principado* (principality) rather than an *autonomía* (autonomous region), and its capital is the city of Oviedo. Its heritage is Celtic, and the heir to the Spanish throne has, since 1388, been styled "Prince of the Asturias," rather as the heir to the British throne has, since 1301, been styled "Prince of Wales." When the Moors ruled most of mainland Spain, Asturias became a reservoir of the Christian royalty of Castilla y León, not to mention the springboard for the revolt that eventually became the *Reconquista*—ultimately, the foundation of a united Spain.

Asturias

The region's prosperity was founded in coal and iron mining, but today its green, cool, mountainous area is rich in pastureland, culminating in the spectacular Picos de Europa, including the 8,738 foot peak of Torrecerredo. The coastline fronts the Bay of Biscay and, along with neighboring Galicia and Cantabria, boasts some of the longest and cleanest beaches in Europe. Gastronomically, it's a seafood region, with particular centers of excellence at Oviedo and Gijón.

LOCAL SPECIALTIES

Cattle farming dominates this almost alpine region and *ternera asturiana* is the beef from the local Asturiana de los Valles and Asturiana de las Montañas breeds, or crosses between them. The cattle lead an almost free-range life in the mountain valleys, are fed on local cereals, vegetables, soy and sunflower seeds, among other produce, during their first five months, and are slaughtered at 12 or 18 months old.

Where there are cattle, there's cheese, and Asturias produces five listed cheeses. The most famous is *Cabrales*, made from raw cow's milk (with an admixture of sheep's and goat's milk) and matured in mountain caves to develop its characteristic blue-green veins. Another is *afuega'l pitu*, which, in the local dialect, means "to choke the chicken." It's a soft cow's-milk cheese; to test its readiness, farmers would feed it to a chicken. If the chicken swallowed it, it was ready to sell. If the chicken choked, it was still too hard. Other cheeses include *beyos*, a hard cow's-milk cheese sometimes with an admixture of goat's and sheep's milk, and lightly smoked; *gamonedo*, a hard cheese, also lightly smoked and made with milk from all three animals; and *vidiago*, a soft, creamy, cow's-milk cheese made in the east of the region.

The "national dish" of Asturias is *fabada Asturiana*, a rich stew made with the local large white *faba Asturiana* (*fava*) beans, *chorizo*, *morcilla* (black pudding), shoulder of pork, and saffron. Despite the humble ingredients, its complex blend of flavors and textures has achieved almost mythical status. Perhaps better than any other dish, this rustic stew exemplifies the simple perfection of traditional Spanish cooking.

Fabada Asturiana

White-bean stew with assorted pork cuts

INGREDIENTS (SERVES 4)

5 cups dried white beans (navy)

10oz pork shoulder

4oz piece of Iberian ham or
   serrano ham

2 *chorizo* sausages, 6 inches long

2 *morcillas* (black puddings),
   6 inches long

1/2 onion

1 carrot

a few strands of saffron

sprigs of flatleaf parsley, to
   garnish (optional)

Soak the beans overnight in plenty of cold water. In another bowl, soak the pork shoulder and ham overnight as well.

Drain the beans and tip into a large saucepan. Cover with fresh cold water. Bring to a boil, then simmer over a low heat for about 1 hour, skimming off any residue that rises to the surface.

After this time, add the rest of the ingredients and cover with more cold water. Bring back to a boil and simmer over a low heat for 2 hours, or until the meats are cooked through. Stir gently from time to time, taking care to keep the beans whole.

Remove the meats, sausages, black puddings, and vegetables from the pan, cut them into small pieces, to produce a mixture known as *compango*, and set aside. Ladle some beans and sauce into deep bowls. Then add a selection of the *compango*. Garnish with sprigs of flatleaf parsley, if desired.

WINE TIPS

SPECIAL OCCASION: **Tares P3, Dominio de Tares, Bierzo (Castilla y León) (€€€)**
SUNDAY LUNCH: **Abadía da Cova Tinto, Moure, Ribeira Sacra (Galicia) (€€)**
EVERYDAY: **Sidra de Asturias (€)**

Asturian food is a model of simplicity, combining fresh locally grown ingredients to produce dishes with remarkably bold flavors. True to form, when the local cider, which is drunk in most *chigres* (bars) in the region, is used to make a sauce for freshly caught hake, the result has a sensationally piquant and original taste. The same sauce works well with any firm white fish.

Merluza a la sidra
Hake with cider sauce

INGREDIENTS (SERVES 4)
8 large clams (shells on)
4 hake fillets
4 shrimp

FOR THE SAUCE
1 tablespoon virgin olive oil
1 onion, finely chopped
2 garlic cloves, finely chopped
1 tablespoon all-purpose flour
1 cup hard cider
2 scallions, finely chopped
salt and freshly ground black
    pepper, to taste

GARNISH
sprigs of parsley
slices of apple, rubbed in lemon
    juice to prevent discoloring

To make the sauce, heat the olive oil in a skillet and fry the onion and garlic gently until soft and golden. Sprinkle in the flour and mix well into the olive oil with a wooden spoon. Pour in the cider, stirring all the time, until the sauce has boiled and is slightly thickened. Just before taking the skillet off the heat, stir in the scallions and season with salt and pepper.

Tip the sauce into a food processor and blend until smooth. Strain the sauce through a sieve and pour it back into the skillet.

Bring back to a boil over a low heat before adding the clams. When the clam shells open, remove from the heat. Discard any clam shells that do not open.

Meanwhile, broil the hake under a medium broiler for 10 minutes. Broil the shrimp for the last 3 minutes.

Spoon a little sauce into the bottom of each dish, then place the hake, 1 shrimp, and 2 clams on top. Garnish with sprigs of parsley and slices of apple.

WINE TIPS
SPECIAL OCCASION: Casal Caeiro Vendimia Seleccionada, Rias Baixas (Galicia) (€€€)
SUNDAY LUNCH: Monasterio de Corias, Vinos Cangas, Cangas (€€)
EVERYDAY: Sidra de Asturias (€)

Roasted meats are very popular in Asturia, especially when served with a cheese sauce, made from the local blue cheese, known as *Cabrales*, or a homemade cheese, such as *afuega'l pitu*, a type of creamy feta-style cheese. Others use plenty of cider in their cooking. This recipe skillfully plays around with traditional ideas to produce a fusion of flavors that would leave any food-lover wanting more.

Cabrito en adobo con patatitas maceradas en reducción de sidra

Marinated kid with new potatoes in a cider sauce

INGREDIENTS (SERVES 4)

3 garlic cloves

fresh parsley, chopped

3lb 5oz kid, on the bone

sprigs of rosemary and thyme

3 tablespoons olive oil

3/4 cup white wine

4oz red *afuega'l pitu* cheese
   or cream cheese

2 eggs, beaten

1/2 cup all-purpose flour

FOR THE SAUCE

2 leeks, chopped

1 onion, chopped

2 carrots, chopped

rosemary, bay, and thyme

2 cups hard cider

FOR THE POTATOES

2 cups hard cider

4 small potatoes, cut in half, with a
   hole in the middle of each piece

4oz *higadillos del cabrito*
   (kid's liver)

Grind the garlic and parsley together in a mortar and pestle to form a paste. Chop the kid into pieces then rub the paste into the kid and allow to marinate for 12 hours in the refrigerator.

Arrange the pieces of kid in an ovenproof dish with the rosemary, thyme, 2 tablespoons of the olive oil, and white wine. Roast in the oven at 250°F for 50 minutes, so that the meat stays moist.

Remove the kid from the oven and allow to cool. When cold, take the meat off the bones and crumble into pieces. Save the bones for making the sauce later. Mix the cheese into the meat and roll into a "sausage" shape. Wrap in plastic wrap and freeze overnight. Cut the meaty cheese sausage into 4 pieces. Dip each piece in the egg, then the flour, and fry over a high heat in lots of olive oil until brown. Set aside.

For the sauce, heat the remaining olive oil in a large saucepan. Tip in the kid bones and brown over a high heat. Throw in the vegetables and herbs, and pour in the cider. Simmer over a very low heat, adding water as required, for 5 hours. Then strain the stock into a clean saucepan. Return to the heat and reduce to a thick glossy sauce.

For the potatoes, bring the cider to a boil in a saucepan, then simmer over a medium heat until reduced by half. Drop in the potatoes and boil for 20 minutes until cooked. Brown the *higadillos del cabrito* in a little olive oil in a skillet, then crush to form a coarse pâté. Carefully stuff the liver pâté into each potato.

Spoon a little cider sauce into each dish. Arrange a kid/cheese roll on one side of the pool and 2 pieces of stuffed potato on the other. Garnish with fresh herbs.

WINE TIPS

SPECIAL OCCASION: **Tilenus Pagos de Posada, Estefanía, Bierzo (Castilla y León) (€€€)**
SUNDAY LUNCH: **Peregrino, Gordonzello, León (Castilla y León) (€€)**
EVERYDAY: **Sidra de Asturias (€)**

In the 15th century, Sephardic Jews brought rice to Asturias. By a happy coincidence, rice goes very well with the creamy local milk to create the region's signature dessert: rice pudding. Traditionally, it is made with just rice and milk, topped with caramel. Introducing cinnamon, star anise, and lemon as well, and the stunning new presentation, adds textures and flavors to tantalize the taste buds.

Arroz con leche Asturiano con helado de canela y crujiente de limón

Rice pudding Asturias-style with cinnamon ice cream and crunchy lemon

INGREDIENTS (SERVES 4)

FOR THE RICE PUDDING
6 tablespoons short-grain rice
6 tablespoons water
4 cups whole milk
1/2 cup heavy cream
grated zest of half an orange
2/3 cup superfine sugar
1/4 cup butter
2 cups whipping cream

FOR THE ANISEED GLAZE
2 cups water
4 star anise
1 teaspoon powdered gelatin

FOR THE ICE CREAM
1 1/3 cups whole milk
1 1/3 cups whipping cream
1/2 cup superfine sugar
2 cinnamon sticks
2 egg yolks
1 teaspoon ground cinnamon

FOR THE CRUNCHY LEMON
1 lemon, very thinly sliced
caramel syrup

For the rice pudding, add the rice to a saucepan with the water, and bring to a boil. Once the water has evaporated, add the milk, cream, and orange zest. Simmer over a low heat for 1 hour, stirring occasionally. Remove from the heat, stir in the sugar and butter, and set aside to cool before putting in the refrigerator.

Whip the cream to a medium stiffness and fold into the cold rice pudding. Pour the rice into a rectangular dish, about 8 x 4 inches and ⅝ inch deep. Put in the refrigerator to set. When ready to roll in the aniseed glaze below, turn the block of creamed rice out onto a cutting board and cut into 4 bars.

For the glaze, boil the water with the star anise and add the gelatin. Pour into a tray to create a thin sheet of jelly and allow to cool before putting in the refrigerator. When set, remove from the tray, cut into 4 strips, and roll around the bars of rice pudding, creating sweet "cannelloni." Trim the ends to neaten and chill until needed.

To make the cinnamon ice cream, put the milk, cream, sugar, and cinnamon sticks in a saucepan. Gently heat to 120°F, stirring to make sure the sugar dissolves. Then beat in the egg yolks and cinnamon. Continue stirring until the temperature rises to 185°F. Remove from the heat and set aside to cool, then pour into a plastic container and put in the freezer until needed.

For the crunchy lemon, soak the lemon slices in caramel syrup then place in the oven at 225°F to dry for 3 hours, or until they are crunchy.

Place a roll of rice and anise glaze "cannelloni" on one side of each dish, and a scoop of cinnamon ice cream on the other. Decorate the ice cream with the crunchy lemon slices. The image shows an optional lemon and lime garnish.

WINE TIPS

SPECIAL OCCASION: **Gallaecia, Martín Códax, Rías Baixas (Galicia) (€€€)**
SUNDAY LUNCH: **Liberalia Uno, Liberalia Enológica, Toro (Castilla y León) (€€)**
EVERYDAY: **Sweet Sidra de Asturias (€)**

Wines of Asturias

Asturias has only one wine area, created in 2001: the Vino de la Tierra de Cangas (www.vinotierracangas.com), in the southwest of the region around the town of Cangas del Narcea. For many years this was an area of domestic winemaking with the odd cottage-industry bodega, but since 2001 some half-dozen bodegas have been making wine on a (usually small) commercial scale. Interestingly, the grapes grown here are mainly unique to Asturias: Albarín Negro, Albarín Blanco (not, they insist, the Albariño of neighboring Galicia), Verdejo Tinto, and Carrasquín Tinto as well as the slightly more familiar Picapoll Blanco, Albillo, Moscatel of Alexandria, and Mencía. Understandably, given the northern climate and seafood culture along the coast of the Bay of Biscay, the whites tend to be better than the reds.

OTHER DRINKS

Asturias is nationally famous for *sidra de Asturias:* i.e. cider (www.sidradeasturias.es). Orchards dominate the northeast of the region, with a concentration along the coast; many cider-apple varieties are unique to Asturias, with names such as Durona de Tresali, Limón Montés, Teórica, Raxao, Xuanina, Fuentes, Verdialona, and Ernestina. Traditionally, the apples are crushed in a wooden trough using wooden mallets and shovels; the juice is then run off into barrels where it ferments for five to seven months. The producer then blends the different barrels to get the right mix of sweetness and acidity before bottling without filtration. Both still and sparkling ciders are made, the latter by natural fermentation in the bottle, and the style is very refreshing (usually quite dry); they are traditionally drunk with *fabada Asturiana.*

Because most traditional ciders have a sediment in the bottle, Asturians have developed a method of pouring called *el escanciado*, which involves holding the bottle horizontally to trap the sediment and pouring from a great height to aerate the cider. This is accomplished by holding the bottle up at arm's length over the head and pouring into a glass held in the other hand. A variation on this is a bodily contortion in which the glass is held behind the back and the bottle poured over the shoulder. It's a matter of skill and great pride to do this without spillage. Some cafés and bars have a mechanism on the wall that does this by pulling a string that tilts the bottle, but this is considered unromantic by traditionalists.

Main Bodegas
(listed in alphabetical order), PRODUCER NAME; town/village; web/E-mail address; best wines (r = red, w = white) A star (*) indicates particularly good quality.

VINOS CANGAS; Cangas del Narcea; www.bodegacorias.com; Monasterio de Corias (w)

Baleares (The Balearic Islands) comprise the inhabited islands (in order of size) of Majorca, Minorca, Ibiza, Formentera, and Cabrera, the last of which is a nature reserve. There are also several small uninhabited islands that are havens for wildlife. Politically, all the islands are grouped together as the province and *autonomía of Illes Balears*.

The Baleares have been a trading post and military base for centuries, although the invaders since the 1960s have had more peaceable ambitions. Well away from the tourist areas, most islands are stunningly beautiful. Majorca has the Serra de Tramuntana ("Mountains of the North Wind") range along its north coast—including the island's

Baleares

highest peak, Puig Major (4,757 feet)—rolling plains in the center (where most of the best vineyards are found), and, of course, small unspoiled fishing ports and dramatic bays with endless beaches. Minorca is the furthest east and has the most beguiling coves and estuaries around its coastline, with a large natural harbor at Mahón, the island's capital and reputedly the birthplace of the now-ubiquitous mayonnaise sauce, known here as *mahonesa*. Ibiza is much smaller but has a cliff-faced coastline with narrow caves on the north coast. Formentera and Cabrera are smaller still, and the nature reserve on Cabrera is only accessible by special permit.

LOCAL SPECIALTIES

The climate is mild and Mediterranean, and the gastronomy very varied. Cheese is a major industry, with *Mahón-Menorca* the most popular, made from raw cow's milk and often rubbed with oil and paprika for extra flavor. Soft when young, it becomes harder with age; Mahón reserva/semicurado is probably the best. Olive oil is a feature of Majorca, made from Mallorquina, Arbequina, and Picual varieties. The oil tends to be fruity when young, aging to a subtle sweetness when mature. Meat products are a major feature, and *sobrassada de Mallorca* is a favorite spicy sausage, rather like chorizo but softer, with a characteristic local flavor. It comes in two styles: *sobrassada* and *sobrassada porc negre*; the latter is made from the meat of black pigs. In the pastry department, the *ensaimada de Mallorca* is made with flour, water, sugar, eggs, and pork lard (everyone has a secret recipe for the amounts), rolled out into a long, thin cylinder, and then wound around into a flat disc before baking. There's a variant that is made as above, but stuffed with angel-hair pasta.

This hearty Mediterranean stew is well loved in the Balearic Islands, especially on Ibiza. An assortment of meats is used in this version but it's just as tasty and nourishing when made with a selection of fish instead. *Bullit* is still enjoyed in two servings: first a bowl of meat, vegetables, and legumes, followed by another of rice. Some *alioli*, a garlic mayonnaise, on the side, livens up the stew no end.

Bullit

Traditional rice stew with assorted meats or fish

INGREDIENTS (SERVES 4)

1¹/₂ cups dried chickpeas

6oz piece of bacon

1 ham bone

1 veal shin bone

1lb 2oz shoulder of lamb,
    off the bone

¹/₂ cabbage, cut into 2 pieces

4 potatoes, peeled and quartered

1 onion, quartered

1 tomato, halved

1 celery stick, chopped

7oz *sobrassada* (Majorcan
    sausage—similar to *chorizo*)

1 *morcilla* (black pudding),
    6 inches long

2¹/₂ cups *calasparra* rice

pinch of saffron

salt, to taste

GARNISH

fried dried red pepper

extra-virgin olive oil with garlic

The night before preparing the stew, put the chickpeas in a bowl of cold water to soak and wash the bacon well.

In a large saucepan, place the bones, lamb, and bacon. Drain the chickpeas and add to the saucepan, then cover with cold water. Bring to a boil, put a lid on the saucepan and allow to cook over a low heat for 2 hours, or until the meats are cooked through. Skim the surface several times during cooking to remove any residue that rises to the surface.

After 2 hours, add the cabbage, potatoes, onion, tomato, and celery. Put the lid back on, return to a boil, and cook for 15 minutes more. Then add the *sobrassada*, *morcilla*, and rice. Replace the lid, bring back to a boil again and cook over a moderate heat for another 15 minutes. Stir in the saffron and salt, reduce the heat to low, and leave for an additional 5 minutes.

Remove the *sobrassada*, *morcilla*, bacon, meats, and vegetables from the pan. Cut the sausages and meat into bite-size pieces.

Serve the stew in the traditional manner—first, bowls of meat, chickpeas, and vegetables garnished with slices of fried dried red pepper, then bowls of rice, seasoned with drizzles of garlic oil.

WINE TIPS

SPECIAL OCCASION: Gran Vinya Son Caules, Miquel Gelabert, Pla i Llevant (€€€)

SUNDAY LUNCH: Buc, Jaume de Puntiró, Binissalem (€€)

EVERYDAY: Macià Batle Añada Tinto, Binissalem (€)

Mahón cheese plays an indispensable part in Minorcan cooking. The square cheeses with their distinctive orange rind have been made by hand on the island for more than 2,000 years. The cheese itself is yellowish, with a firm texture and the slightly sweet taste of fresh milk. As this simple recipe proves, it's best eaten on its own or with some ham, tomatoes, and olives—and plenty of fresh crusty bread.

Queso fresco de Mahón con jamón Ibérico, tomates secos con olivas y albahaca

Fresh Mahón cheese with Iberian ham and dried tomatoes with olives and basil

INGREDIENTS (SERVES 4)

FOR THE CHEESE AND HAM
2 cups heavy cream
9oz fresh Mahón cheese
5 sheets of leaf gelatin, soaked
7oz Iberian ham or *serrano* ham, sliced very thinly and finely shredded

FOR THE DRIED TOMATOES
10 tomatoes
dash of extra-virgin olive oil
dash of Sherry wine vinegar
salt, to taste
pinch of sugar

FOR THE OLIVE AND BASIL OIL
1 cup black olives
1 bunch of fresh basil
1 cup olive oil

GARNISH
pitted black olives, sliced
fresh basil leaves

For the cheese and ham, pour the cream into a saucepan and bring to a boil. Remove the orange rind from the cheese, cut into small cubes, and stir into the hot cream. Return to a boil, take off the heat, and add the gelatin, stirring until the leaves dissolve.

Blend the mixture in a food processor and then strain through a sieve into a bowl. Allow to cool, before putting in the refrigerator for 6 hours to set. Then grate the creamy cheese block and set aside.

For the dried tomatoes, scald and peel the tomatoes. Cut in half and seed. Put in a large baking dish and sprinkle with the olive oil, vinegar, salt, and sugar. Place in the oven at 225°F to dry for 3 hours.

For the olive and basil oil, pit the olives and wash the basil. Blend the olives, basil, and olive oil in a food processor to form a smooth runny paste.

Arrange 2 heaps of grated cheese on opposite sides of each plate with a pile of ham in between. Place a dried tomato between each pile and drizzle a little olive and basil oil around the plates. Garnish with sliced olives and fresh basil leaves.

WINE TIPS

SPECIAL OCCASION: **Stairway to Heaven, Castell Miquel, Tramuntana-Costa Nord (€€€)**
SUNDAY LUNCH: **Sió, Ribas, Illes Balears (€€)**
EVERYDAY: **Crianza Franca Roja, José L Ferrer, Binissalem (€)**

Sobrassada (Majorcan sausage) has to be *the* taste of Majorca. This cured sausage, made from meat and pork fat, seasoned with paprika, and similar local sausages, such as *longanizas, culanas,* and *bisbe,* are practically the only regular source of meat in the Majorcan diet. Dishes of fresh meat are saved for special occasions. Here, *sobrassada* is served in appetizing partnership with fresh shrimp and sweet, juicy mangoes.

Broceta de gambas con sobrassada Mallorquina y vinagreta de mangoy

Shrimp kebabs with Majorcan sobrassada and mango salsa

INGREDIENTS (SERVES 4)

14oz *sobrassada* or *chorizo*
    sausages cut into small cubes

FOR THE KEBABS

20 large raw shrimp
olive oil for frying
salt, to taste

FOR THE SALSA

2 mangoes, peeled and
    finely diced
4 shallots, peeled and
    finely chopped
8 tablespoons sunflower oil
salt, to taste

GARNISH

edible flower petals—from
    marigolds, nasturtiums, or roses
4 red sorrel leaves
4 red Swiss chard leaves
oil for frying

Peel and devein the shrimp, and remove the heads. Thread 5 shrimp onto each of 4 skewers and brown in a little olive oil in a skillet over a medium heat for about 2 minutes, turning once, until pale pink all over. Add a pinch of salt to taste.

For the salsa, mix the mangoes and shallots together thoroughly in a bowl. Stir in the sunflower oil and a pinch of salt. Leave in the refrigerator for 3 hours to let the flavors blend. Then drain off the surplus oil.

In a skillet, briefly submerge the flower petals and red sorrel and red Swiss chard leaves in hot oil over a high heat until crisp.

Spoon some well-drained mango salsa onto each plate. On one side, place a pile of sausage cubes and on the other, the skewered shrimp. Sprinkle a little mango salsa over the top. Garnish with the flower petals and fried leaves.

WINE TIPS

SPECIAL OCCASION: **Miquel Gelabert Selecció Privada, Pla i Llevant (€€€)**
SUNDAY LUNCH: **Can Majoral Galdent Viognier, Pla i Llevant (€€)**
EVERYDAY: **Vinya Son Fangoz, Toni Gelabert, Pla i Llevant (€)**

Throughout the Balearics, the traditional dishes of the islands reflect the influence of various cultures over many centuries. This *cuscussó*, for example, is a dessert with Arabic roots and an age-old Minorcan specialty, which is particularly popular at Christmas time. The recipe makes excellent use of the wonderful crisp almonds, juicy dried fruit, and heavenly scented lemons grown on the island.

Cuscussó Menorquín
Almond and lemon-peel cake, Minorca-style

INGREDIENTS (SERVES 4)
2 cups granulated sugar

3/4 cup water

3/4 cup lard

1 tablespoon raisins, soaked for 30 minutes in water

1/2 teaspoon cinnamon

1 teaspoon finely grated lemon zest

1lb 2oz dried crusty bread, crushed into fine bread crumbs (7 cups)

13/4 cups blanched almonds, finely chopped

2 ready-to-eat dried figs, very finely chopped

2 ready-to-eat dried apricots, very finely chopped

DECORATION
2 tablespoons pine nuts, lightly toasted under the broiler

2 tablespoons raisins

Put the sugar in a saucepan and pour in the water. Stir over a low heat with a wooden spoon until the sugar dissolves.

Raise the heat to medium and stir in the lard, raisins, cinnamon, and lemon zest.

When the lard has melted, mix in the bread crumbs, almonds, figs, and apricots. Stir over a medium heat for about 5 minutes, then beat vigorously with a wooden spoon, working the mixture until the *cuscussó* is elastic and pliable, with a consistency similar to marzipan. Add more water if necessary.

Pack the *cuscussó* into a shallow rectangular dish, or form into 12 small balls by rolling the mixture between the palms, and set aside to cool. Before serving, turn the *cuscussó* out of the dish and cut into 12 bars.

Put 3 bars or balls of *cuscussó* onto each plate. Decorate with a few pine nuts and raisins over the top.

WINE TIPS
SPECIAL OCCASION: **Palo de Mallorca (€€€)**
SUNDAY LUNCH: **Can Rich Dulce, Ibiza/Eivissa (€€)**
EVERYDAY: **Original Muscat, Miquel Oliver, Pla i Llevant (€)**

Wines of Baleares

The first DO, Binissalem-Mallorca, was created in Majorca in 1991 and in the early days, bodegas concentrated on local grapes: Manto Negro and Callet for reds, Moll for whites. Since then experiments with Cabernet Sauvignon, Merlot, Syrah, and Chardonnay have changed the face of island viticulture. Binissalem is a fairly tightly concentrated area in the center of the island, and it was joined by a second DO area called Pla i Llevant de Mallorca (literally "plain and east coast of Majorca") in 2001. This effectively covers the southeastern half of the island. The result has been quite a spectacular improvement in the island's wines.

DO BINISSALEM-MALLORCA

This is the heart of Majorca's winemaking area. Manto Negro grapes for red wines and Moll (also known as Prensal) for whites are still an important part of the mix, but international varieties are now present in most vineyards.

DO PLA I LLEVANT DE MALLORCA

A very large area, not all of which is under vine. Although the local grapes are cultivated, there is also a great deal of experimentation with international varieties. Quality is generally very high.

OTHER WINES

VdlT Illes Balears A region-wide country wine allowing winemakers more flexibility in what they produce. These range from the everyday to some quite spectacular wines made by bodegas that simply refuse to conform.

VdlT Tramuntana-Costa Nord The northwest half of Majorca, with vineyards running up to the northern mountain range. In this way the whole of the island is covered by a DO or VdlT wine classification.

VdlT Ibiza and VdlT Isla de Menorca Recent island-wide classifications. Some potential, but most of the wine goes into the local tourist trade.

OTHER DRINKS

Palo de Mallorca is an old-fashioned local liqueur made by infusing grape spirit with quinine, gentian, sugar, and caramel. The result is dark, almost black in color with flavors of licorice and caramel, and a slightly bitter finish. It is usually drunk as a *digestivo*.

Main Bodegas

(listed in alphabetical order), PRODUCER NAME; town/village;
web/E-mail address; best wines (r = red, w = white, p = pink)
A star (*) indicates particularly good quality.

DO BINISSALEM-MALLORCA
www.binissalemdo.com

JAUME DE PUNTIRO; Santa María del Camí;
www.vinsjaumedepuntiro.com; Buc (r), JP (r)*

JOSE L FERRER; Binissalem; www.vinosferrer.com; Veritas (w),
José Ferrer (r), D2UES (r)*

MACIA BATLE; Santa María del Camí; www.maciabatle.com;
Pagos de María (r)*

DO PLA I LLEVANT DE MALLORCA
www.plaillevantmallorca.es

MIQUEL GELABERT; Manacor; www.vinsmiquelgelabert.com;
Chardonnay (w)*, Gran Vinya Son Caules (r)*

MIQUEL OLIVER; Petra; www.miqueloliver.com; Ses Ferritges
(r), Aía (r)*

PERE SEDA; Manacor; www.pereseda.com; Pere Seda (r, w, p),
Gvivm (r)*

TONI GELABERT; Manacor; www.vinstonigelabert.com;
Chardonnay (w)*, Vinyes Velles (r)*

VdlT ILLES BALEARS

AN NEGRA; Felanitx; anegra@hotmail.com; Àn (r)*

RIBAS; Consell; www.bodegasribas.com; Sió (r)*

VdlT TRAMUNTANA-COSTA NORD

CASTELL MIQUEL; Alaró; www.castellmiquel.es; Stairway to
Heaven (r)*

Canarias (The Canary Islands) are an archipelago of seven islands formed from dormant or extinct volcanoes, approximately 68 miles east of the north African coast. Under the 1978 Spanish constitution, Canarias became an *autonomía* in its own right, divided into two provinces: Santa Cruz de Tenerife, which includes the islands of Tenerife, La Gomera, El Hierro, and La Palma; and Las Palmas de Gran Canaria, which includes the islands of Lanzarote, Fuerteventura, and Gran Canaria. All the islands produce some wine, with the exception of Fuerteventura, and the main industries are tourism, construction, and agriculture in approximately equal thirds. Perhaps the most beguiling island is Lanzarote, where in 1730 a

Canarias

volcanic eruption covered the island in lava, which solidified to produce black soil, black landscapes, and even black sand on the beaches.

Historically, the islands have been important as a strategic base in the Atlantic Ocean, especially during the exploration of the New World as a supplies stop for ships on their way to South America. They prospered greatly, especially during the boom in the market for *sack*, the sweet, fortified wine based on the styles of wine from Jerez (Sherry) in Andalucía.

LOCAL SPECIALTIES

Fruit and vegetables are the main products of all the islands, and Canarias potatoes (known locally as *papas*) were always the harbinger of summer in northern Europe when they arrived in the spring. Canarias tomatoes have always been a major winter crop and Canarias onions are still an important part of the agricultural economy. Probably the biggest fruit crop is bananas, and the island of La Palma seems to be an endless carpet of velvet-green banana palms. Local restaurants have an infinite number of ways of doing different things with bananas on their dessert menus.

Each island has its own cheeses, but two have made their mark nationally: *queso majorero* is made on Fuerteventura from goat's milk with a little sheep's milk. It's a semihard cheese and comes "fresh" (softer) or *semicurado* (harder). *Queso Palmero* is made from the milk of the long-horned goats of La Palma and is lightly smoked and soft to the touch. There's also a local bread called *gofio*, which is traditionally made from wheat flour, barley, corn, or chickpeas, which are roasted and then mixed with water or milk to form a kind of paste that can be baked to taste. Sometimes vegetables (particularly legumes) may be added to the mix.

Canarias boasts tropical temperatures that are ideal for growing more exotic fruits than in the rest of Spain, including avocados, papayas, mangoes, guavas, pineapples, and bananas. These feature regularly in the islands' cuisine, enlivened with aromatic herbs and spices. This recipe for *vieja*, a sea fish with a coarse scaly skin and tender white flesh, combines the best of the local produce in an original way.

Vieja a la parilla con crema de papaya y cilantro

Broiled fish with papaya cream and fresh cilantro

INGREDIENTS (SERVES 4)

4 *viejas*, or sea bream, each
    weighing about 1lb 9oz
olive oil
salt, to taste

FOR THE SAUCE

⅔ cup peeled and roughly
    chopped papaya
⅓ cup superfine sugar
juice of 1 lemon
1 cup fresh cilantro
⅔ cup heavy cream
2 eggs

GARNISH

purple basil or cilantro (optional)
edible flower petals—nasturtium,
    marigold, or rose (optional)
balls scooped from melon and
    mango (optional)

Clean and fillet the fish, removing all the bones.

For the sauce, blend the papaya with the sugar and lemon juice in a food processor. Strain the puree through a sieve into a bowl and set aside in the refrigerator.

Blanch the cilantro in a saucepan of boiling water. Then blend the cilantro and cooking water together in a food processor. Set aside.

Make a custard by heating the cream to boiling point. Then remove from the heat and set aside to cool slightly. Beat the eggs and sugar together in a bowl. When the cream is warm rather than hot, beat in the egg and sugar mixture. Return the saucepan to the heat and stir continuously with a wooden spoon over a low heat until the custard thickens. Then stir in the cilantro juice and set aside to cool.

When the cilantro custard is cool, stir in the papaya puree with a spatula.

Brush the fish fillets with olive oil and season with a little salt. Put the fish under a medium broiler and cook for about 5 minutes on each side until golden.

Spoon some papaya and cilantro custard onto each plate, and then put a piece of fish on top. Drizzle over a few drops of olive oil. Garnish with a sprig of purple basil/cilantro, a sprinkling of edible flower petals, and a few melon and mango balls, if desired.

WINE TIPS

SPECIAL OCCASION: **Brumas de Ayosa Brut Nature (sparkling), Comarcal, Valle de Güímar (€€€)**
SUNDAY LUNCH: **Viñátigo Gual Blanco, Ycoden-Daute-Isora (€€)**
EVERYDAY: **Gran Tehyda Blanco, Valleoro, Valle de la Orotava (€)**

The *papas* (potatoes) of the Canarias are small and sweet, and the mainstay of the islands' economy and cuisine. Today many varieties are cultivated and any of them can be used to create this fragrant, spicy dish. The name comes from the way the potato skins wrinkle up when cooked in salty water—originally in sea water—and from its *mojo* (sauce) of chili peppers and cumin seeds.

Papas arrugadas con mojo picón
Wrinkled potatoes with a spicy cumin sauce

INGREDIENTS (SERVES 4)

2lb 4oz Canarias potatoes or small
    new potatoes (the thicker the
    skins, the better)

4 tablespoons salt

FOR THE SPICY SAUCE

2 chili peppers, seeded and
    finely chopped

1 garlic clove, peeled and chopped

salt and pepper, to taste

1 tablespoon ground cumin

1 slice crisp fried white bread,
    crusts cut off, chopped into
    small squares

1 teaspoon paprika

1 cup olive oil

4 tablespoons vinegar or to taste

Wash the potatoes, but don't peel them. Tip into a flameproof casserole, cover with cold water, and add the salt. Bring to a boil over a high heat, then reduce the heat to low. Cover the casserole with foil, then put the lid on top. Gently boil the potatoes until all the water has evaporated. Keep a close eye on the water level to make sure the potatoes don't burn dry. Remove the lid and foil, and leave the potatoes in the casserole over a low heat until the skins wrinkle and develop a salty crust. Set aside.

To prepare the sauce, place the chilies, garlic, salt, pepper, and cumin in a mortar and crush together with a pestle to form a smooth paste. Add the fried bread and continue crushing. Then mix in the paprika and drizzle in the olive oil, little by little as if making mayonnaise, stirring continuously. Then add the vinegar to taste.

Trim an end of each potato to form a flat base and cut a shallow cross in the other end. Squeeze gently below the cuts to open out the top a little and spoon in a teaspoon of spicy sauce. Stand all the potatoes in a serving dish and serve as an accompaniment.

WINE TIPS

SPECIAL OCCASION: **Monje Listán Negro, Tacoronte-Acentejo (€€€)**
SUNDAY LUNCH: **Viña Norte Barrica, Insulares Tenerife, Tacoronte-Acentejo (€€)**
EVERYDAY: **Hoyo de Mazo Tinto, El Hoyo, La Palma (€)**

The *Guanches*, the original inhabitants of the Canarias, had a simple but nutritious diet based on a mixture of stone-ground and toasted cereals called *gofio*. This coarse flour has survived, pretty much unchanged, to the present day. This thick porridge-like soup, which can be eaten for breakfast, is a fine example of the numerous sweet and savory recipes that feature the delicious, characteristic flavor of *gofio*.

Sopa de gofio

Roasted corn, wheat, and rye soup

INGREDIENTS (SERVES 4)

1/2 cup olive oil

1 onion, finely chopped

6 tablespoons *gofio*: a coarse flour of ground, roasted corn, rye, and wheat grains

salt, to taste

herb oil, to garnish (optional)

Heat the olive oil in a skillet over a medium heat. Tip in the onion and sauté until transparent. Add the *gofio* and stir with a wooden spoon to form a smooth toasted paste.

Boil a kettle. When the water is hot but not boiling, slowly start adding tablespoonfuls to the skillet, until the ball of *gofio* becomes a smooth runny porridge. Season with a little salt and simmer over a low heat until thickened.

Spoon some *gofio* soup into each bowl. Garnish with few drops of herb oil, if desired.

WINE TIPS

SPECIAL OCCASION: El Grifo Malvasía Fermentado en Barrica, Lanzarote (€€€)
SUNDAY LUNCH: Viñátigo Marmajuela Blanco, Ycoden-Daute-Isora (€€)
EVERYDAY: El Lomo Blanco, AFECAN, Tacoronte-Acentejo (€)

Malvasía grapes make one of the most prized wines of the Canarias, "Canary Sack." As a regular consumer of the divine nectar, Robert Louis Stevenson may well have been referring to Canary Sack when he wrote "Wine is bottled poetry." Today, a strong, sweet Malvasía wine is perfect for revitalizing *bienmesabe*: a traditional paste of dried fruits, nuts, and egg, similar to marzipan.

Bienmesabe con velo de chocolate blanco y granizado de vino de Malvasía

Egg, almond, and sugar paste with a white chocolate crust and Malvasía ice

INGREDIENTS (SERVES 4)

FOR THE *BIENMESABE*

6 tablespoons mineral water
3 tablespoons superfine sugar
13/4 cups blanched almonds, toasted and finely chopped
1/2 cup sweet Malvasía wine
4 egg yolks, beaten in 2 tablespoons of milk
finely grated zest of 1 lemon
1 teaspoon ground cinnamon

FOR THE CRUST

4oz white chocolate, broken into small pieces

FOR THE ICED DRINK

1 cup sweet Malvasía wine

DECORATION

2/3 cup Pedro Ximénez dessert wine, reduced to 2 tablespoonfuls (optional)

Prepare a light syrup by warming the water and sugar in a saucepan over a low heat, stirring carefully until the sugar dissolves. Then add the almonds, stirring continuously with a wooden spoon over a low heat for about 10 minutes. Add the wine, the eggy milk, lemon zest, and cinnamon. Continue to stir continuously until a smooth paste forms. Set aside to cool.

For the white chocolate crust, melt the chocolate pieces in a bowl over a saucepan of simmering water. Spread the melted chocolate over a piece of parchment paper lining a baking sheet with a spatula to create a very thin, even sheet of white chocolate. Briefly chill in the refrigerator until barely hard, then stamp out discs with a round, 2½ inch, straight-edged cookie cutter.

For the iced drink, pour the wine into a saucepan and heat over a medium heat until reduced by half in volume. Pour into a plastic container and set aside to cool before putting in the freezer to ice up.

Spoon some of the iced Malvasía wine into 4 glasses. Place a spoonful of the *bienmesabe* on top, then position a white chocolate disc on top of that. Decorate with the reduction of PX (Pedro Ximénez) dessert wine drizzled over the top, if desired.

WINE TIPS

SPECIAL OCCASION: **Malvasía Dulce, El Grifo, Lanzarote (€€€)**
SUNDAY LUNCH: **Humboldt, Insulares Tenerife, Tacoronte-Acentejo (€€)**
EVERYDAY: **El Grifo Canari Malvasía, Lanzarote (€)**

Wines of Canarias

The Canarias have no fewer than 11 *denominación* wines spread over six of the seven islands. The range is wide, and the sweet, fortified wines known in Shakespeare's time as "Canary Sack" are still made from Malvasía, Pedro Ximénez, and Moscatel grapes, particularly on Lanzarote. Main red varieties are Listán Negro and Negramoll. Most interesting, perhaps, are some ancient varieties, long forgotten on the mainland, which still survive on the islands. They include Burrablanca, Breval, Diego, Almuñeco, Sabro, Gual Bermejuela, Forastera Blanca, and Vijariego, but the more serious areas are also planting Tempranillo, Cabernet Sauvignon, and Merlot. Styles tend to be light and fresh, made for early drinking and largely directed at the tourist trade. Few bodegas have the capacity to export as far as the Iberian peninsula (715 miles) let alone to the international market. For general information, see www.bodegacanaria.com.

DO AREAS ON TENERIFE

DO Abona This area occupies the southern quarter of the island, centered around the town of Arico, with vineyards as high as 2,953 feet toward the volcanic crater. They grow most of the island's varieties and make young wines for the tourist trade.

DO Tacoronte-Acentejo On the island's northern tip, this is one area that is able to export and has the quality wines with which to do it: mainly reds from Listán Negro and sweet whites from Malvasía.

DO Valle de Güímar A small area around the town of Güímar on the east coast of the island, with vineyards planted at up to 4,921 feet. Mainly white-wine grapes (Listán Banco) with some red from Listán Negro.

DO Valle de la Orotava Another small area, directly opposite Valle de Güímar on the west side of the island, making mainly fruity white wines from Listán, Gual, and Vijariego.

DO Ycoden-Daute-Isora On the southwestern tip of the island, this area is perhaps most famous for the dragon tree of Icod, which is at least 1,000 years old and possibly more.

Wines are largely white, both sweet (Malvasía, Moscatel) and dry (native Canarias varieties).

DO AREAS ON GRAN CANARIA

DO Monte Lentiscal Very small area around Santa Brígida, in the northeast of the island. The best wines tend to be reds made from Listán Negro from the highest vineyards; up to 2,625 feet.

DO Gran Canaria A more recent DO (2000) that takes in all the rest of the island apart from Monte Lentiscal. Mostly light, fruity reds from Listán Negro for immediate drinking, and largely sold into the tourist industry.

ISLAND-WIDE DOs

DO Lanzarote Vineyards here are excavated from black volcanic soil and protected from the prevailing winds by walls that have been built around individual vines. Small-scale at present, but makes some of the best traditional Canarias sweet wines from Malvasía.

DO La Palma This beautiful island makes all kinds of wine, but mainly sweet whites in the traditional Canarias style, from Malvasía grapes. There is some good red from Negramoll.

DO La Gomera The most recent DO (2004) in the islands, making mainly light, fresh, young wines, principally warm, fleshy whites from the Forastera grape.

DO El Hierro Makes mainly sweet whites from Moscatel and Pedro Ximénez.

OTHER WINES
The smoky, misty, subtropical north highlands of the island of La Palma make wines called *Vino de Tea*, which don't have a DO but do have a big local following. *Tea* in this instance is the Spanish word for a type of pine from which vats and barrels are made, adding a certain piquancy to the flavor. The wines are then aged for many years in caves excavated in the mountainsides until they oxidize and turn almost black: a style known on mainland Spain as *rancio* (literally "rancid"). It's not exactly a commercial product, but people who like this sort of thing usually find that it's something they enjoy... mainly on La Palma.

Main Bodegas
(listed in alphabetical order), PRODUCER NAME; town/village; web/E-mail address; best wines (r = red, w = white, p = pink) A star (*) indicates particularly good quality.

DO ABONA
crdoabona@worldonline.es

CUMBRES DE ABONA; Arico; cumbresabona@wanadoo.es; Cumbres de Abona (r, w, p)

DO TACORONTE-ACENTEJO
www.tacovin.com

EL LOMO; Tegueste; www.bodegaellomo.com; El Lomo (r, w)

INSULARES TENERIFE; Tacoronte; www.bodegasinsularestenerife.es; Viña Norte (r)

MONJE; El Sauzal; www.bodegasmonje.com; Monje (r)

DO VALLE DE GUIMAR
www.vinosvalleguimar.com

COMARCAL VALLE DE GUIMAR; Arafo; www.bodegacomarcalguimar.com; Brumas de Ayosa (r, w, p)

DO VALLE DE LA OROTAVA
www.dovalleorotava.com

VALLEORO; La Orotava; www.bodegavalleoro.com; Gran Tehyda (r, w)

DO YCODEN-DAUTE-ISORA
www.ycoden.com

VINA DONIA; Miradero y Ancón Icod; www.bodegasinsularestenerife; El Ancón (r)

VIÑÁTIGO; La Guancha; www.vinatigo.com; Viñátigo (r, w)

DO MONTE LENTISCAL
montelentiscal@telefonica.net

DO GRAN CANARIA
crdogc@terra.es

DO LANZAROTE
www.dolanzarote.com

EL GRIFO; San Bartolomé de Lanzarote; www.elgrifo.com; El Grifo (w)*

DO LA PALMA
www.malvasiadelapalma.com

EL HOYO; Villa de Mazo; www.bodegaselhoyo.com; Hoyo de Mazo (r, w)

DO LA GOMERA
www.fundacionalhondiga.org/crgomera.php

DO EL HIERRO
www.elhierro.tv/crdo

antabria is one of the most beautiful parts of Spain, with green landscapes, a craggy coastline, some of Europe's cleanest beaches, and a large slice of the breathtaking Picos de Europa. The capital is Santander, a major port during the exploration of the New World, and today still a center for shipping, trade, and car ferries. It's an *autonomía* consisting of a single province: one of the most prosperous in the north of Spain, and one of the leading consumers of wines from elsewhere in the country, although it has no classified vineyards of its own.

The city suffered a massive fire and gale-force winds in a storm in 1941, which destroyed much of its ancient architecture—including the splendid Romanesque

Cantabria

cathedral (only the crypt remains)—as the fire burned for two days. There were, fortunately, very few fatalities, but thousands of families were left homeless, and much of the modern city dates from the 1950s onwards. As one of the most northerly cities of Spain, it remains a popular destination for Spanish people escaping the summer heat of the south.

LOCAL SPECIALTIES

Understandably, with a coastline along the Bay of Biscay, the local gastronomy relies heavily on fish—particularly angler fish, sea bass, sole, and turbot, but also sardines, anchovies, mackerel, and tuna, along with squid, often served up as a fish stew with potatoes. Shellfish, including *percebes* (goose foot barnacles; *see* Galicia, page 118) and everything from shrimp to lobster, spiny crab to clams, can be found in seafront restaurants along the coast.

This lush green landscape is also cattle country, however, and *carne de Cantabria* (Cantabrian beef) is one of the great specialties of the region. The cattle breeds are Alpine Brown, Tudanca, and Monchina, bred and raised in the highland pastures, and slaughtered and butchered in the highlands.

There are three protected cheeses from Cantabria. *Picón bejes-tresviso* is a blue cheese from the Liébana region, southeast of the Picos de Europa national park. It's made mainly with cow's milk, but is often blended with some sheep's and goat's milk, depending on what style the cheesemaker wants: creamy or sharper. *Quesucos de liébana* is a white version of the same cheese from the same area, slightly softer and occasionally smoked. *Queso de Cantabria* is a generic cheese made all over the province from cow's milk. It's soft and creamy when young, harder and sharper when mature.

Although Cantabria is better known for its exceptional seafood, the region also produces simple, honest dishes featuring more humble ingredients. One specialty from the coastal area of Laredo is *respigos* (turnip leaves), which are much admired for their slightly hot, peppery flavor. When cooked well, they can accompany any dish, however grand, although pairing the greens with crispy bacon works beautifully.

Respigos de carbón con panceta de cerdo
Sweet chargrilled turnip greens with bacon

INGREDIENTS (SERVES 4)

1lb 2oz piece of bacon

2 leeks, roughly chopped

1 onion, roughly chopped

3 carrots, roughly chopped

1 garlic clove

3 handfuls *respigos* (turnip greens) or collard greens

salt, to taste

olive oil, for deep-frying

GARNISH

sea salt flakes (optional)

sprouting seeds (optional)

Place the bacon, vegetables (except the greens), and garlic in a large saucepan. Cover with cold water and put a lid over the top. Bring to a boil over a high heat and allow to simmer over a low heat for at least 6 hours, to produce a flavorsome stock for a sauce.

While the bacon is cooking, wash the greens well. Bring plenty of water to a boil over a high heat in a large saucepan. Plunge the greens into the water and boil for about 15 minutes. Carefully pour off the boiling water and rinse the leaves under cold running water to cool them down quickly. Lay individual leaves on the grill over the heat of a charcoal barbecue and season with a little salt. (The greens can be finished off under the broiler, but never seem to taste quite as good.)

When the bacon is cooked through, remove from the saucepan and cut the piece into 4 cubes. Deep-fry each cube in plenty of olive oil until crispy.

Meanwhile, blend the stock and vegetables together in a food processor. Strain through a sieve to create a smooth sauce.

Pour a little sauce into each dish, then put a cube of the fried bacon on top and arrange a portion of the greens alongside. Garnish the bacon with a few flakes of sea salt, and a handful of sprouting seeds, if desired.

WINE TIPS

SPECIAL OCCASION: áster reserva, Ribera del Duero (Castilla y León) (€€€)

SUNDAY LUNCH: Valdelosfrailes Prestigio, Cigales (Castilla y León) (€€)

EVERYDAY: Altos de Tamarón, Pagos del Rey, Ribera del Duero (Castilla y León) (€)

Cantabria is the most important anchovy-canning region in Spain. During the canning process, the fish are cleaned, salted, and preserved. The salty little fillets that emerge from the can are invaluable for creating numerous snacks, appetizers, seafood tapas, and sauces. Because it's always so useful to have a supply of anchovies to hand, this recipe demonstrates how straightforward it is to prepare and preserve the fresh fish.

Anchoas en conserva
Preserved north-coast anchovies

INGREDIENTS (SERVES 4)
2lb 4oz fresh anchovies
plenty of coarse sea salt
oregano, to taste
paprika, to taste
ground black pepper
1/2 cup superfine sugar
extra-virgin olive oil

Clean the anchovies well, removing the heads and guts. It's a delicate task, because the fish should be handled as little as possible, and then only with cold hands. Slit down the back of each fish, separating and boning the fillets, and set aside. (Alternatively, ask a fishmonger to do this.)

Combine the rest of the ingredients, except the olive oil, to make the seasoning. Place a layer of the sweet, spiced salt in the bottom of a large shallow dish. Then arrange a layer of the fish on top and finish with another layer of seasoning.

Leave the dish in the refrigerator for about 2 hours, then transfer the anchovies to a large glass jar, or plastic container, and cover in extra-virgin olive oil. Keep the fish under oil in the refrigerator for up to 3 months.

Every time you want to use the anchovies, wash the fillets well to remove the seasoning and revive with a drizzle of fresh olive oil.

WINE TIPS
SPECIAL OCCASION: Quinta Apolonia Verdejo, Belondrade, Castilla y León (€€€)
SUNDAY LUNCH: LB Gewurztraminer, Luna Beberide, Castilla y León (€€)
EVERYDAY: Txacoli Eizaguirre, Getariako Txakolina (País Vasco) (€)

Like many popular recipes in Cantabria and the Basque country, the identity of exactly who first thought of cooking *jibiones* (squid) in their own ink is lost in the mists of time. This dramatic dish of rice cooked in a dark, aromatic sauce, served with squid and mushrooms, is an exciting blend of flavors from land and sea, and certainly rates highly among the great culinary delicacies of northern Spain.

Jibiones asados con arroz negro y boletus
Barbecued Basque squid with black rice and ceps

INGREDIENTS (SERVES 4)
4 *jibiones* (squid), cleaned
    and dried

FOR THE RICE
1³/4 cups short-grain rice
    (*calasparra* and *arborio*
    are suitable)
3 cups fish stock
2 bags squid ink
splash of light cream

FOR THE CEPS
2 large fresh ceps, sliced
extra-virgin olive oil

GARNISH
olive oil
chives

Cook the rice in a large saucepan with 2 cups of the fish stock and all the ink for about 10 minutes until half-cooked. Transfer the rice to another saucepan, pour in the remaining fish stock, bring to a boil and cook for about 6 minutes. At the end of cooking, stir in a little cream to sweeten the rice.

Preheat the oven to 140°F. Arrange the mushroom slices on a baking sheet, drizzle over some olive oil and roast in the oven for 25 minutes until soft.

Preheat the oven to 350°F. Brown the squid under a medium broiler for 15 minutes, then transfer to a baking sheet and finish cooking in the oven for 3 minutes.

Spoon a little black rice into each bowl, then lay 2 or 3 slices of mushroom on the rice, and balance a roasted squid on top. Garnish with a drizzle of olive oil and 2 chives.

WINE TIPS

SPECIAL OCCASION: Naiades, Naia, Rueda (Castilla y León) (€€€)
SUNDAY LUNCH: Palacio de Bornos Vendimia Seleccionada Sauvignon, Rueda (Castilla y León) (€€)
EVERYDAY: Quinto Hinojal, Casto Pequeño, Castilla y León (€)

Blue cheese is a staple of the northern Spanish diet. In Tresviso, *picón* cheese is produced to an ancient formula, which is closely guarded by the local shepherds. Made with sheep's milk for creaminess, cow's milk to support the blue veining, and goat's milk for its strong taste, the flavor and intensity of *picón* are unforgettable. In this recipe, the cheese is just one of several distinguished Cantabrian flavors used.

Emulsión de alubias rojas con buñuelo de queso Picón y lomo de boquerón macerado en especias

Creamed kidney beans with blue-cheese fritters and spiced anchovy fillets

INGREDIENTS (SERVES 4)

7oz fresh anchovies

1 teaspoon salt

1/2 teaspoon each of ground black pepper, ground white pepper, dried oregano, dried thyme, and dried rosemary

2 bay leaves

6 tablespoons olive oil

1 1/2 tablespoons wine vinegar

FOR THE KIDNEY BEANS

1 3/4 cups red kidney beans

1 onion

1 garlic clove

2 teaspoons cayenne pepper

olive oil

salt, to taste

FOR THE FRITTERS

4oz *picón*, or blue cheese

1 3/4 cups all-purpose flour

2 tablespoons beer

salt, to taste

olive oil, for batter and for drizzling

Clean and fillet the anchovies (*see* page 66). Plunge the fillets into cold water, drain, and dry well on kitchen towel. Arrange in a single layer in a shallow dish. Combine the salt, peppers, herbs, olive oil, and vinegar to make a marinade for the anchovies, and pour over the fish. Place in the refrigerator for 24 hours. Rinse and dry each fillet before serving.

Soak the kidney beans in plenty of cold water overnight.

Bring a large saucepan of water to a boil. Drain the soaked kidney beans, tip into the boiling water and add the onion, garlic, and cayenne. Bring back to a boil, then cook over a high heat for 15 minutes. Turn the heat down to medium and continue boiling for at least another 45 minutes, or until the beans are soft. Then drain and put the bean mixture in a food processor and blend until creamy. Pour in as much olive oil as needed to loosen the consistency. Add salt to taste.

For the fritters, mold the cheese into 12 small balls and set aside in the refrigerator. Mix together the flour, beer, a little salt, and enough oil to make a thick batter. Roll the balls of cheese in the batter and fry in lots of hot olive oil. Carefully remove from the oil with a slotted spoon, then drain on some kitchen towel.

Spoon some red kidney bean puree onto each plate. Arrange 3 cheese fritters on top and some anchovies on the side. Garnish with a drizzle of olive oil.

WINE TIPS

SPECIAL OCCASION: **Luna Beberide Reserva, Castilla y León (€€€)**
SUNDAY LUNCH: **Vagal Pago de Ardalejos, Castilla y León (€€)**
EVERYDAY: **Casar de Burbia Tinto, Bierzo (Castilla y León) (€)**

Wines of Cantabria

There are no classified wines in Cantabria, but the Liébana region (of cheese fame; *see* page 62) makes a modest local wine. There are fewer than 50 hectares under vine, mostly divided into small plots, many of them domestic in size and ambition. They grow Mencía and Tempranillo for red wines, Palomino and Verdejo for whites, and total production might peak at 250,000 bottles per year, a good deal of which may be sold off for distillation into *orujo* (*see* below).

CANTABRIA BODEGAS

There are a few small bodegas that have ambitions to win promotion to vino de la tierra status, but commercial production would initially be very small, in the region of just 60,000 bottles per year. There is an even smaller industry for the production of sweet wines made from dried grapes (with thereby concentrated sugars), fermented for two weeks in oak vats. They are known generically as tostadillos.

There is also an unofficial classification for wines of the "Costa de Cantabria." Some nine hectares produce about 40,000 bottles a year of white wines made from Albariño, Hondarribi Zuri, Godello, Riesling, and Chardonnay. None of these wines has any official status or is seen outside the region.

OTHER DRINKS

Although winemaking is on a very small scale, there is an equally small distilling industry making *orujo de Cantabria*. However, the issue is rather fudged as there is no *denominación*, and pomace from neighboring regions can be imported for distillation in Cantabria. Some spirits are infused with honey or herbs to make a sweet liqueur. None of these drinks have any official classification as yet.

Along with its neighbors Asturias to the west and the Basque Country to the east, Cantabria has a cider industry, although it isn't as well developed on an industrial scale. Most production is on a domestic level, but there's a good deal of tradition and there is a *cofradía de la sidra de Cantabria* ("Cantabrian cider brotherhood"), which holds its own cider festivals.

Castilla y León is Spain's largest region, with nine provinces: Ávila, Burgos, León, Palencia, Salamanca, Segovia, Soria, Valladolid, and Zamora. The cities have been variously capitals, seats of government, universities, cathedrals, myths, and legends. It is the heartland of Castile, and was the base from which Castilian forces fought the Moors in the 11th century. It's the land of El Cid and Queen Isabella, who married Ferdinand of Aragón to lay the foundations of a united Spain.

LOCAL SPECIALTIES

It's not surprising that Spain's largest region also has the widest variety of local produce: almost everything Spain produces can be found here in one form or another. Beef products include *carne de Ávila, de Cervera y de la Montaña Palentina* (Palencia), *de Morucha de Salamanca, de Pinares-El Valle* (Soria and Burgos), *ternera de Aliste* (Zamora), *del Bierzo* (León), and *ternera charra* (Salamanca), all farmed in the

Castilla y León

rural pastures of their various provinces. Lamb is important, too: *lechazo de Castilla y León* is milk-fed lamb from all over the region, with a particular specialty being *lechazo Montañas del Teleno* from León. Pork products range from the *cochinillo de Segovia* and *jamón guijuelo* (Salamanca), as well as *embutidos* (sausages), especially *chorizo de Cantimpalos* (Segovia), *morcilla de Burgos, botillos del Bierzo,* and *cecina de León:* air-, sun-, or smoke-dried sausage.

Cheeses include *queso Castellano,* a hard variety with a nutty flavor which is made all over the region except the province of Zamora, which has its own *queso Zamorano.* Burgos also has its own cheese, softer than Castellano, and usually eaten young and fresh. All these are made with cow's milk. Other cheeses include *queso de Villalón* (Valladolid), which is a sheep's milk cheese, and *queso de Valdeón* (León), a strong blue cheese made from cow's and goat's milk.

Fruit and vegetables are equally varied: León has the *Manzana Reineta del Bierzo,* a special variety of apple that comes in both green and russet. Legumes are widespread: *garbanzos* (chickpeas) *de Fuentesaúco* come from Zamora and *judías del Barco de Ávila* and *alubias de la Bañeza-León* are white and colored beans; lentils, too—*lentejas de la Armuña* (Salamanca) and *lentejas pardina de Tierra de Campos* are grown in the northern part of the region. Sweet peppers are grown in León; the *pimiento asado del Bierzo* has been around since the 1650s, and *pimientos Fresno-Benavente* are red sweet peppers grown in León and Palencia.

Spanish sausages are famous for their variety and quantity, and one of the most valued is the *botillo* of León. In many ways it is a typical sausage, made of pig's ribs and tail, seasoned with salt, paprika, and garlic, smoked and dried, but its size is not typical—it usually weighs about 3¾ lb. This large sausage makes numerous traditional dishes in this region—hearty, simple, and nourishing.

Botillo Leonés
Round pork sausage with cabbage and potatoes

INGREDIENTS (SERVES 4)
1 *botillo*, weighing 2lb 4oz
1lb 12oz green cabbage
salt, to taste
1lb 12oz potatoes
deep-fried sorrel leaves,
    to garnish (optional)

Put the *botillo* in a saucepan and cover with water. Bring to a boil over a high heat, cover with a lid, then cook over a medium heat for about 1 hour until tender.

Wash and shred the cabbage, and add to the saucepan. Add a little salt, bring back to a boil over a high heat, then simmer over a low heat for about 30 minutes.

Peel the potatoes and cut into large, irregular pieces. Add to the saucepan and cook over a medium heat for about 20 minutes until well cooked.

Cut up the *botillo* and serve in bowls, accompanied by the cabbage, potatoes, and cooking liquid. Garnish with deep-fried sorrel leaves, if desired.

WINE TIPS
SPECIAL OCCASION: **San Román, Maurodós, Toro (€€€)**
SUNDAY LUNCH: **Pago de Ardalejos, Vagal, Castilla y León (€€)**
EVERYDAY: **Peregrino Tinto, Gordonzello, León (€)**

The farming region of Salamanca is famous for its pastures and chanfaina is a lamb stew that, like paella, has many variations in style and ingredients. The essential ingredient is lamb and the dish traditionally includes all parts of the animal. The dish originates from shepherds, who would make good use of the less attractive parts of the animal in order to prepare this stew. This version of the dish uses only lambs' feet.

Chanfaina

Lamb stew with bay leaves, garlic, hot pepper, and white wine

INGREDIENTS (SERVES 4)

8 lambs' feet
2 tablespoons olive oil
1 onion, halved and sliced
3 garlic cloves
2 bunches of parsley
1 clove
pinch of nutmeg
1 teaspoon salt
3/4 tablespoon freshly ground
   black pepper
1 tablespoon all-purpose flour

GARNISH

2 red bell peppers, roasted
2 eggs, hard-cooked and sliced

Carefully clean the lambs' feet and put in a large saucepan. Cover with cold water and bring to a boil over a high heat, then cook over a medium heat for 1 hour. From time to time, skim off any residue that rises to the surface.

Heat the olive oil in a skillet and sauté the onion for 10 minutes. Grind the garlic, parsley, clove, nutmeg, salt, and pepper to a paste in a mortar with a pestle. Stir into the skillet with a wooden spoon.

Transfer the meat from the saucepan to a flameproof casserole, saving the meat stock to use later. Tip in the contents of the skillet. Sprinkle the flour over the meat, onion, and seasonings, and stir in some of the reserved meat stock. Simmer over a low heat for 2 hours, until the meat is tender and cooked through.

Serve the stew in bowls, garnished with roasted peppers and hard-cooked eggs.

WINE TIPS

SPECIAL OCCASION: **Aalto, Ribera del Duero (€€€)**
SUNDAY LUNCH: **Arzuaga Crianza, Arzuaga Navarro, Ribera del Duero (€€)**
EVERYDAY: **La Legua, Emeterio Fernández, Cigales (€)**

Scented, thick, and firm, the fresh mushrooms used in this recipe are from the *boletus* family and are a celebration for the taste buds. Here they provide the ideal ingredient when accompanied by a good duck's liver, with a red wine sauce. They are a typical delicacy in the fall, when you can eat them fresh.

Tarrina de boletus y foie macerado en vino tinto

Terrine of ceps and duck's liver marinated in red wine

INGREDIENTS (SERVES 4)

1lb 2oz ceps (mushrooms), sliced
salt, to taste
olive oil, for drizzling
8 sheets of leaf gelatin, soaked in
    cold water
12oz fresh duck's liver
8 cups red wine
1 tablespoon superfine sugar

Preheat the oven to 225°F. Spread the mushrooms on a baking sheet, sprinkle on some salt and a drizzle of olive oil. Roast the mushrooms in the oven for 30 minutes. Drain any liquid from the mushrooms into a bowl and, while still warm, stir in the gelatin until dissolved. Add the mushrooms to the liquid and spoon into 4 silicon muffin molds or 4 compartments of a nonstick muffin pan, to make tub-shaped mushroom jellies. Set aside to cool before leaving in the refrigerator overnight.

Cover the duck's liver with 2½ cups red wine and marinate for 24 hours. Then drain off the wine and brown the liver under a medium broiler until cooked through.

Pour the remaining wine into a saucepan and add the sugar. Heat gently over a medium heat, stirring until the sugar dissolves. Then boil to reduce the wine until there is about ⅔ cup left in the saucepan.

Unmold the mushroom jellies and put one on each plate. Place some duck's liver beside the mushrooms and pour over the wine reduction.

WINE TIPS

SPECIAL OCCASION: **Pintia, Toro (€€€)**
SUNDAY LUNCH: **Dominio de Tares Cepas Viejas, Bierzo (€€)**
EVERYDAY: **Altos de Tamarón, Pagos del Rey, Ribera del Duero (€)**

These sweet handmade spheres, yellow in color and with the texture of a melting and delicate egg yolk, are an example of how a few ingredients can produce a sublime dessert. Some say they are of Arab origin, although they owe their popularity to the Order of the Carmelites and to one of their most famous nuns, St. Teresa of Jesus. With the saffron cream and almond crust of this recipe, they are irresistible.

Yemas de Santa Teresa sobre cremoso de azafrán y crujiente de almendra

Sweet egg yolks with saffron cream and almond crust

INGREDIENTS (SERVES 4)

FOR THE DOUGH
1 cup granulated sugar
1 cup boiling water
11 eggs, separated, plus
   1 whole egg
grated zest of 1 lemon
¼ cup superfine sugar
confectioners' sugar

FOR THE SAFFRON CREAM
2 eggs
2 tablespoons granulated sugar
6 tablespoons heavy cream
pinch of saffron
¼ cup butter

FOR THE ALMOND CRUST
½ cup granulated sugar
½ cup boiling water
1¾ cups ground almonds

DECORATION
1 tablespoon confectioners' sugar

For the dough, put the granulated sugar and water in a saucepan and cook, stirring, over a low heat until the sugar dissolves to make a syrup. Allow to cool for 10 minutes, then beat the egg yolks, one at a time, into the syrup, finally adding the whole egg and lemon zest. Return to the heat and cook gently, stirring constantly with a wooden spoon, until the yolks set.

Sprinkle the superfine sugar onto a work surface and pour out the resulting dough on top. Allow to cool and then form the dough into small balls between your palms. Roll the balls in the confectioners' sugar and set aside for serving.

For the saffron cream, mix the eggs and sugar together. Add the cream and the saffron and boil in a pan, stirring well so that it does not stick. Then remove from the heat and add the butter, before straining through a fine sieve. Allow to cool and set aside for serving.

For the almond crust, preheat the oven to 350°F. Put the sugar in a bowl, pour over the water, and stir until the sugar has dissolved. Set aside to cool. Then beat in the ground almonds. Line a baking sheet with parchment paper and spread the sweet almond paste thinly over the tray. Bake in the oven for 5 minutes, then remove and pat out the crust by hand. Set aside to cool.

Spoon some saffron cream onto each plate and arrange 3 dough balls on top. Lay a piece of the almond crust beside the balls. Decorate with a dusting of confectioners' sugar.

WINE TIPS

SPECIAL OCCASION: **Flor del Saúco Ora Pro Nobis, Vega Saúco, Toro (€€€)**
SUNDAY LUNCH: **Bornos Sauvignon Dulce, Castilla La Vieja, Rueda (€€)**
EVERYDAY: **Castel Ámbar, Castelo de Medina, Rueda (€)**

Wines of Castilla y León

Castilla y León has an enviable reputation for quality wines, largely due to the success of the Ribera del Duero DO and the Tinto Fino grape (also known as Tinto del País: it's actually the local variant of Tempranillo). Although the wine-producing areas tend to follow the course of the River Duero as it wends its way toward the Portuguese border, there are highland vineyards here up to 2,953 feet, with well-drained soils, high in chalk content and ideal for growing vines. At altitude, the sun is hot in the ripening season but the temperature drop at night can be as much as 30 degrees, allowing the vine to "sleep" rather than continue using up nutrients in the soil needed by the grape during the day. The only white wine of note is made in Rueda from Verdejo and, latterly, Sauvignon Blanc, a contender (along with the Albariño of Rías Baixas; *see* Galicia, page 126) for the title of "classic white wine of Spain."

Castilla y León is also the first region to implement the new (2003) VCPRD category. The letters stand for *Vinos de Calidad Producido en Regiones Determinadas*—"quality wines produced in specific regions"—the EU-wide classification for quality wines.

DO BIERZO

In the province of León, this is the home of the "difficult" Mencía grape, which had too much acidity until it was tamed by Álvaro Palacios at Corullón. Since then (1999) investment has flooded into Bierzo, which is now making some wonderful wines.

DO CIGALES

Cigales is north of the city of Valladolid, and is a region well known for making rosado (rosé) wines, even though reds are its best, mainly Tempranillo. Soils are well drained with large stones, and the potential is excellent.

DO RIBERA DEL DUERO

The DO that started Castilla y León on the quality trail. Although the region's oldest bodega (Vega Sicilia) dates back to 1864, it was 1982 before the DO was granted, and it was Alejandro Fernández of Pesquera who lit the flame with his 1986 vintage. The main grape is Tinto Fino, the style is concentrated, powerful, and perfumed.

DO RUEDA

Historically, Rueda made fortified, Sherry-type wines because the local Verdejo grape oxidized so quickly that unfortified wines were stale before they got into the bottle. Francisco Hurtado de Amezaga of Marqués de Riscal (Rioja) discovered that, when handled properly, Verdejo could produce wonderful, fresh, crisp, clean white wines. Today, they pick at night and transport the grapes under inert gas to protect them from air. Riscal also introduced Sauvignon Blanc into the region. Red wines were admitted in 2001, but whites still dominate.

DO TORO

Toro has a reputation for big, blockbusting reds made from Tinto de Toro (Tempranillo). The land is hot and high, up to 2,789 feet, and grapes ripen comfortably without fear of damage by frosts.

VCPRD WINES

Five regions were all promoted from *Vino de la Tierra* to quality-wine status in 2005.

VCPRD Arlanza This straddles the border between Palencia and Burgos and is mainly planted with Tinto del País, Mencía, Garnacha, and Cabernet Sauvignon, with Viura and Albillo for whites, though most production is of red.

VCPRD Arribes This follows the course of the River Duero southward on the western edge of the provinces of Zamora and Salamanca. They grow the local Juan García and Rufete, as well as Tempranillo and Garnacha.

VCRPD Tieras de León In the south of the province of León they grow the local Prieto Picudo grape along with Mencía and Tempranillo for mainly red-wine production. There is some Palomino and Verdejo for white.

VCRPD Valles de Benavente This area neighbors Tierras de León (*see* above), but across the border in Zamora. They grow the same mix of grapes, although there's more emphasis on Tempranillo for future quality wines.

VRCPD Zamora Quite a large area with some vineyards over the southern border in Salamanca, growing mainly Tempranillo, Garnacha, and Cabernet Sauvignon with a small amount of white-wine grapes. Once again, reds are better—quite surprisingly good in some cases.

OTHER WINES

VdlT de Castilla y León Created to give flexibility to winemakers and growers who wanted to plant something different. Some of the region's best wines come under this classification.

In addition there are registered VdlT zones in Cebreros (Ávila), Sierra de Salamanca, and Valtiendas (Segovia), but many bodegas are gradually migrating to the VdlT de Castilla y León or one of the VCPRD areas if they meet the criteria.

Main Bodegas
**(listed in alphabetical order), PRODUCER NAME; town/village;
web/E-mail address; best wines (r = red, w = white, p = pink)**
A star (*) indicates particularly good quality.

DO BIERZO
www.crdobierzo.es

CASAR DE BURBIA; Carraceledo; www.casardeburbia.com;
Casar de Burbia (r), Hombros (r)

DESCENDIENTES DE J PALACIOS; Villafranca del Bierzo;
bodega@djpalacios.com; Petalos del Bierzo (r), Corullón (r)*

DOMINIO DE TARES; San Román de Bembibre;
www.dominiodetares.com; Bembimbre (r)*, Tares P3 (r)*

ESTEFANIA; Ponferrada; www.tilenus.com; Tilenus (r), Pagos
de Posada (r)*

PEIQUE; Valtuille de Abajo; www.bodegaspeique.com;
Peique (r)

PRADA A TOPE; Cacabelos; www.pradaatope.es; Palacio de
Canedo (r)

DO CIGALES
www.do-cigales.es

CESAR PRINCIPE; Fuensaldaña; 983-583-242; César PrÍncipe (r)*

EMETERIO FERNANDEZ; Fuensaldaña; www.lalegua.com; La
Legua (r), La Legua Capricho (r)*

LEZCANO LACALLE; Trigueros del Valle;
www.bodegaslezcano.com; Lezcano Lacalle

VALDELOSFRAILES; Cubillas Santa Marta;
www.matarromera.es; Valdelosfrailes

DO RIBERA DEL DUERO
www.riberadelduero.es

AALTO; Roa de Duero; www.aalto.es; Aalto (r)*, Aalto PS (r)*

ALEJANDRO FERNANDEZ; Pesquera;
www.grupopesquera.com; Alenza (r)*, Pesquera Janus (r)*

ALION; Padilla de Duero; www.bodegasalion.com; Alión (r)*

DOMINIO DE PINGUS; Quintanilla de Onésimo; 983-680-189;
Flor de Pingus(r)*, Pingus (r)*

EMILIO MORO; Pesquera de Duero; www.emiliomoro.com;
EmilioMoro, Malleolus (r)*

MATARROMERA; Valbuena; www.matarromera.es;
Matarromera (r)*

MONASTERIO; Pesquera; www.haciendamonasterio.com;
Hacienda Monasterio Reserva Especial (r)*

PAGOS DEL INFANTE; Quintanilla de Onésimo;
pagosdelinfante@usuarios.retecal.es; Lynus (r)*,
Lynus Aurea (r)*

RENACIMIENTO; Olivares de Duero; www.matarromera.es;
Rento (r)*

RODERO; Pedrosa de Duero; www.bodegasrodero.com;
Carmelo Rodero (r)*, Viñas de Valtarreña (r)*

TELMO RODRIGUEZ; Logroño; cia@fer.es; Matallana (r)*,
M2 de Matallana (r)*

VEGA SICILIA; Valbuena; www.vega-sicilia.com; Valbuena (r)*,
Unico (r)*

DO RUEDA
www.dorueda.com

AGRICOLA CASTELLANA; La Seca;
www.agricolacastellana.com; Azumbre (w)*, Cuatro Rayas (w)

ALVAREZ Y DIEZ; Nava del Rey; Mantel Blanco (w)*

DOS VICTORIAS; San Román de la Hornija;
www.dosvictorias.com; José Pariente (w)*

HERMANOS DEL VILLAR; Rueda; www.orodecastilla.com; Oro
de Castilla Verdejo (w)

J & F LURTON; Santiuste de San Juan Bautista;
www.jflurton.com; Hermanos Lurton (w)*

MARQUES DE RISCAL; Rueda; www.marquesderiscal.com;
Marqués de Riscal Verdejo (w)*

NAIA; La Seca; bodegasnaia@terra.es; Naia (w)*

PALACIO DE BORNOS; Rueda; www.palaciodebornos.com;
Palacio de Bornos Verdejo (w)

VEGA DE LA REINA; Rueda; www.vegadelareina.com; Vega de la Reina Verdejo (w)*

VERACRUZ; Pozáldez; b.veracruz@terra.es; Ermita Veracruz (w)*

DO TORO
www.dotoro.es

FARINA; Toro; www.bodegasfarina.com; Gran Colegiata (r), Campus (r)*

J & F LURTON; Toro; www.jflurton.com; Campo Elisio (r)*, Toro El Albar (r)*

LIBERALIA ENOLOGICA; Toro; www.liberalia.es; Liberalia (r), Paciencia de Barnard Magrez (r)*

MAURODOS; Villaester; www.bodegasmauro.com; San Román (r)*

NUMANTHIA TERMES; Valdefinjas; www.eguren.com; Numanthia (r)*

REJADORADA; Toro; www.rejadorada.com; Sango de Rejadorada (r)*, Rejadorada Roble (r)*

VCPRD ARLANZA

HIJOS DE MAXIMO ORTIZ GONZALEZ; Covarrubias; Viña Valdable (r)

LA COLEGIADA; Lerma; www.bodegalacolegiada.com; Lerma (r)

VCPRD ARRIBES

HACIENDAS DURIUS-VALLE; Fermoselle; www.haciendas-espana.com; Durius (r), Durius Magister (r)*

LA SETERA; Fornillos de Fermoselle; www.lasetera.com; La Setera Juan García (r)

VCPRD TIERRAS DE LEÓN

GORDONZELLO; Gordoncillo; www.gordonzello.com; Peregrino (r, w)

VCPRD VALLES DE BENAVENTE

OTERO; Benavente; www.bodegasotero.com; Valleoscuro (r, w, p)

VCPRD ZAMORA

ALIZAN; Moreleja del Vino; www.alizan.net; Alizán Élite (r)

EL CENIT; Villanueva del Campeán; victore@telefonica.net; Cenit (r)*

VdlT DE CASTILLA Y LEON

ABADIA RETUERTA; Sardón de Duero; www.abadia-retuerta.com; Pago Negralada (r)*, Selección Especial (r)*

BELONDRADE; La Seca; belondrade@vodafone.es; Quinta Apolonia (w)*

DEHESA DE RUBIALES; Fuentes de Ropel; www.galiciano.com; Polivarietal (r)*, Prieto Picudo (r)

FERNANDEZ RIVERA; Vadillo de la Guareña; www.grupopesquera.com; Dehesa la Granja (r)

LEDA VINAS VIEJAS; Tudela de Duero; www.bodegasleda.com; Leda Viñas Viejas (r)*

LUNA BEBERIDE; Cacabelos; www.lunabeberide.com; Luna Beberide (r)*

MAURO; Tudela de Duero; www.bodegasmauro.com; Vendimia Seleccionada (r)*, Terreus (r)*

VAGAL; Valtiendas; www.vagal.es; Pago de Ardalejos (r)*

When the Moors were driven back to Granada, the forces of Castilla y León (Old Castile) recaptured the vast plains south of Madrid (including La Mancha) and subsequently recolonized them with Castilian people who had been driven out during the Moorish occupation, creating Castilla-La Mancha (New Castile). Land concessions meant that many people took advantage of the opportunity to set up their own smallholdings. After the establishment of Madrid as the national capital by King Felipe II in 1561, there were opportunities for these smallholders to do business. The king built a 124-mile road from Madrid to Granada, the southern capital, recently vacated by the Moors, to speed the royal mails, troops, churchmen, and dignitaries; this passed through the provinces of Toledo and Ciudad Real. In those days the journey would have taken two or three days, so the highly paid government officers needed food, wine, and accommodation along the way, and the local farmers grew the food and the grapes, made the oil, wine, and the cheese.

Perhaps this explains why *queso Manchego* is Spain's most popular cheese, even after five centuries.

Castilla-La Mancha

Today the *autonomía* of Castilla-La Mancha has five provinces: Toledo and Ciudad Real to the south of Madrid, Albacete to the east, and Cuenca and Guadalajara east of Madrid.

LOCAL SPECIALTIES

Queso Manchego is made all over the region from sheep's milk. It comes *fresco*, fresh and soft to the touch; *curado*, a harder version, slightly crumbly; and *viejo*, aged and often marinated in olive oil until it turns nearly black. It's often served with *membrillo*, a quince jelly. Other livestock products include *cordero* (lamb) and *lechal* (milk-fed lamb). The lamb comes from 391 named villages through the five provinces, and the sheep are of the local Manchega breed; everything from feed to environment and even transport is covered by a regulatory body.

In the market gardens, eggplants from Almagro (Ciudad Real), *ajo morado* (purple garlic) from Las Pedroñeras (Cuenca), and melons from La Mancha (Ciudad Real) are all protected, as are olive oil from the mountains of Toledo and the Campo de Montiel (Ciudad Real). In the sweet department, there's honey from La Alcarria (Guadalajara) and marzipan from Toledo. The most expensive product, as ever anywhere in the world, is *azafrán* (saffron) *de la Mancha*, which is harvested in six *comarcas* (counties). Don't even ask the price.

FRANCESAS 2'40 €

3'50

MORANA 2'70 €

FABES

HABAS 2'40 €

PINTAS DE LEON 2'40 €

FUENTESABOR

HABAS PELADAS 2'85 € Kilo

PEDROSIL 2'40 €

SALAMANCA 2'90 €

LENTEJAS PELADAS 2'85 €

SECOS 1'80 €

FRIJOLES 2'40 €

CARILLAS 2'40 €

The 16th and 17th centuries were the most creative period in Spanish court cookery. Cervantes and Lope de Vega describe in detail the fabulous dishes produced by marrying new foods from America with native ingredients. Partridge from Toledo played a leading role in royal banquets. This modern interpretation updates the age-old flavors with an earthy taste of mushrooms and the sweetness of plums.

Perdiz a la Toledana en diferentes texturas, con escabeche de hongos y frutas de hueso

Partridge Toledo-style with glazed ceps and plums

INGREDIENTS (SERVES 4)
3 tablespoons olive oil
4 partridges, cleaned well
2 onions, finely chopped
4 carrots, cut into sticks
1 garlic clove, chopped
1 bay leaf
2 cups water
2 cups red wine
2 cups white wine
salt and pepper, to taste
1lb 2oz ceps (mushrooms), sliced
olive oil to coat ceps
1lb 2oz plums, pitted and cut into
    1/4 inch slices

FOR THE SYRUP
3/4 cup water
1 cup sugar

GARNISH
sprigs of fresh rosemary
1/2 cup fresh red currants

Heat 3 tablespoons of olive oil in a skillet over a medium heat. Put the partridges in the skillet and brown all over, turning halfway through the cooking time. Transfer the birds to a pressure cooker and stew for 40 minutes, or until cooked through.

In the same skillet brown the onions, carrots, and garlic over a low heat for 8 minutes. Then tip the vegetables into the pressure cooker. Toss in the bay leaf and cover the partridges and vegetables with the water, and red and white wine. Add salt and pepper, put on the lid, bring to a boil, and cook for 15 minutes.

Preheat the oven to 225°F. Put the ceps in a large bowl, season with salt and pepper, and toss in enough olive oil to coat each slice lightly. Spread out the slices on a baking sheet and cook in the oven for 30 minutes.

Meanwhile, to make a syrup for the plums, pour the water and sugar into a saucepan and bring to a boil over a medium heat, stirring constantly until the sugar has dissolved. Raise the heat and boil until the syrup thickens. Add the plums to the syrup and boil for 5 minutes. Remove from the heat and stir in the ceps.

Transfer the partridges to a cutting board and quarter each bird: remove the legs and take the breasts off the bone. To make a sauce, strain some of the cooking juices from the pressure cooker into a saucepan and boil over a medium heat until thickened and glossy.

Spoon some glazed mushrooms and plums onto each plate. Arrange two breasts and legs on top, or sit a whole partridge on the plate. Pour a decorative trail of the sauce around the plate. Garnish with a sprig of fresh rosemary and fresh red currants.

WINE TIPS
SPECIAL OCCASION: **Emeritus, Dominio de Valdepusa, DO Pago** (€€€)
SUNDAY LUNCH: **El Vínculo, Alejandro Fernández, La Mancha** (€€)
EVERYDAY: **Vega Moragona Alta Selección, La Magdalena, Ribera del Júcar** (€)

In days gone by, shepherds used to eat a hearty meal like this to keep up their strength while moving their flocks from summer to winter pastures and back again in the spring. This is a lighter version, but it will still warm you up even on the coldest winter days, especially when accompanied by lots of crusty bread and a good Spanish wine.

Gachas manchegas

Almorta flour paste with bacon, garlic, and paprika

INGREDIENTS (SERVES 4)

4 large potatoes, chopped

1 onion, finely sliced

1 bay leaf

salt, to taste

3 or 4 tablespoons extra-virgin
    olive oil

4 garlic cloves, chopped

1 tablespoon paprika

2 tablespoons *almorta* flour

8 eggs

truffle oil

7oz slices of Canadian bacon,
    rind removed

Put the potatoes, onion, bay leaf, and salt into a saucepan and cover with cold water. Place a lid on the saucepan and boil over a high heat for about 20 minutes. Then drain the potatoes and onion, and discard the bay leaf.

Meanwhile, heat 2 tablespoons of the olive oil in a skillet and fry the garlic until golden. Stir the paprika and *almorta* flour into the olive oil with a wooden spoon and cook until toasted. Set aside.

In a saucepan of gently simmering water, lightly poach 4 of the eggs. Put the poached eggs, the contents of the skillet, and the drained potatoes and onion into a food processor. Blend to a very creamy consistency, adding 1 or 2 tablespoons of extra-virgin olive oil as required. Pour into a saucepan and warm very gently over a low heat until hot, but don't let the potato puree boil.

Separate the remaining 4 eggs, carefully wrapping each yolk individually in a little bag made from plastic wrap. Add a pinch of salt and a few drops of truffle oil to each, then seal with tightly knotted cooking string. Cook in a saucepan of boiling water for about 2½ minutes, then remove the bags from the water and set aside to cool.

Whiz the bacon in a food processor until pulverized.

Arrange a mound of bacon in the base of each soup bowl. Then carefully unwrap a truffle-infused egg yolk and place on top. Pour in the hot creamy potato puree until it covers the bacon and half submerges the yolk, then serve immediately.

WINE TIPS

SPECIAL OCCASION: **Finca Antigua Reserva, La Mancha (€€€)**
SUNDAY LUNCH: **Pago de la Jaraba Crianza, La Mancha (€€)**
EVERYDAY: **Castillo de Almansa, Piqueras, Almansa (€)**

A humble dish of bread cubes or crumbs, *migas* formed the staple diet of the peasants in La Mancha, as well as Andalucía, Extremadura, and Navarra. Consequently, it's possible to find recipes calling for such diverse ingredients as herring, eggs, grapes, even pomegranates. This *migas* comes from rural La Mancha and is probably the most authentic. It's quick to prepare and tastes marvelous after a long walk in the fresh air.

Migas del pastor
Pan-fried bread cubes with an assortment of meats

INGREDIENTS (SERVES 4)
2lb 4oz day-old bread

salt, to taste

5 tablespoons paprika

5 tablespoons virgin olive oil

1 garlic clove, finely chopped

1lb 2oz bacon, diced

1lb 2oz *chorizo* sausages, diced

Cut the bread into ¼ inch cubes and place in a bowl. Toss with the salt and paprika and cover with a damp cloth.

Heat the olive oil in a skillet and sauté the garlic. When golden, add the bacon, and then the *chorizo*. Once the bacon and chorizo are crisp and brown, add the bread cubes and fry, stirring continuously, so that the bread becomes crisp too, but doesn't get greasy.

Put a portion of *migas* on each plate and serve immediately.

WINE TIPS
SPECIAL OCCASION: **Arrayán Premium, La Verdosa, Méntrida (€€€)**
SUNDAY LUNCH: **Ruiz Villanueva Syrah, Bruno Ruiz, Castilla (€€)**
EVERYDAY: **Viña Albali, Félix Solís, Valdepeñas (€)**

A soft paste of almonds and sugar called marzipan was introduced to Spain by the Arabs in the 12th century, and proved particularly popular in Castile, Aragón, and Granada. Today, it's still enjoyed in many almond-producing regions and features in many recipes. This light, smooth version is complemented by the freshness of the lemon verbena and a touch of licorice.

Esponja de mazapán con sorbete de hierba luisa y crujiente de regaliz

Marzipan sponge with lemon verbena sorbet and licorice crunch

INGREDIENTS (SERVES 4)

FOR THE MARZIPAN SPONGE

1 1/3 cups superfine sugar

1 3/4 cups ground almonds

2 egg whites

1 egg yolk

2 cups water

6 sheets of leaf gelatin, soaked
    in cold water

FOR THE LEMON VERBENA SORBET

4 cups lemon verbena leaves

1 cup water

1 cup superfine sugar

1 1/2 teaspoons stabilizer

FOR THE LICORICE CRUNCH

4 egg whites

1 3/4 cups confectioners' sugar

1/3 cup butter, creamed with
    1 teaspoon licorice extract

DECORATION

confectioners' sugar, for dusting
    (optional)

For the marzipan sponge, mix the superfine sugar with the ground almonds in a bowl. Lightly beat the egg whites and yolk together and pour, little by little, into the ground almonds, stirring constantly, to form a paste. Put the almond paste in a saucepan with the water and gelatin. Warm over a low heat for about 10 minutes, stirring all the time, until the gelatin has dissolved in a smooth marzipan "soup." Don't let the mixture boil. Pour into a bowl and allow to cool, then put in the refrigerator for about 12 hours to set.

Once cooled, blend the marzipan jelly in a food processor or mixer, then use a whisk to increase its volume and make it lighter. Form the mixture into a cylinder and cut into 4 portions.

For the lemon verbena sorbet, infuse the lemon verbena leaves with 1 cup hot water for 2 hours. Then mix 1 cup of the infusion with the sugar and stabilizer. Pour into a plastic container and put in the freezer for about 10 hours.

For the licorice crunch, preheat the oven to 350°F and line a baking sheet with parchment paper. Beat the egg whites until stiff, then gradually add the sugar to form a meringue. Gently fold the meringue into the licorice butter until evenly distributed. Then spread the mixture onto the sheet and bake in the oven for 5 minutes until brown. Allow to cool for 2 minutes, and while still soft stamp out 4 disks with a cookie cutter.

Put a piece of the marzipan sponge on one side of each plate and a scoop of the lemon verbena sorbet on the other. Decorate with the licorice crunch and dust with confectioners' sugar, if desired.

WINE TIPS

SPECIAL OCCASION: **Corte Dulce, Pago del Vicario, Castilla (€€€)**
SUNDAY LUNCH: **S & G Dulce Natural Tinto, Vinícola de Castilla, La Mancha (€€)**
EVERYDAY: **Viña Albali Dulce, Félix Solís, Valdepeñas (€)**

Los "Huevos Rotos"
Los "Huevos Morcillones"
El Revuelto "Habanero"
Las Tortillas { Triqueros
                Habas
                Melva
                Tag...

Oregano
Melva

Wines of Castilla-La Mancha

Castilla-La Mancha has rocketed from the obscurity of mass-market, low-cost, everyday wines to become one of the most dynamic and exciting regions of Spain. Low land prices attracted investment from the 1980s onward, and these hot, high vineyards (1,969–2,297 feet) have few problems with insect pests and fungal diseases. They grew a great deal of the white Airén and the red Cencibel (the local name for Tempranillo) and very little else, but this was to change radically. Vinícola de Castilla was the first to invest serious money in the La Mancha DO in the 1970s; after a slow start, others followed. The local government pioneered the region-wide VdlT de Castilla in 1999/2000 and also created the mechanism to establish pago DOs. These are single estates (*pagos*) of international reputation, usually not within mainstream DO areas, which have the right to make wines in their own way. The prime mover in the campaign for these was Carlos Falcó, the Marqués de Griñón, of Dominio de Valdepusa (*see* page 94). To date there are only three DO *pagos* in Spain, all in Castilla-La Mancha, with a possible fourth waiting in the wings (Finca Guijoso, Sánchez Muliterno, *see* page 95). The pago DO concept was enshrined in the new national wine law of 2003.

Castilla-La Mancha also pioneered incremental DO areas within the giant La Mancha DO. After years of debate about whether La Mancha was simply too big, two areas within it that have a reputation for consistently higher-level winemaking were identified, and Ribera del Júcar and Uclés were established in 2001 and 2006, respectively. Bodegas can make wine from certified vineyards under the individual DO names, or blend wines and market them as DO La Mancha.

Today, Castilla-La Mancha makes everything from the humblest everyday wines by the local cooperative to world-class wines from individual estates, with everything in between. It is a veritable winemaking powerhouse, driving quality, individuality, and value for money.

DO ALMANSA

This is in Albacete, but almost an enclave within the neighboring DO Alicante and growing Monastrell grapes like its neighbors to the south in Murcia: Jumilla, and Yecla. For several years, just one bodega (*see* page 95) has been carrying the flag for Almansa, and doing it well.

DO DEHESA DEL CARRIZAL (PAGO)

This single estate in the Montes de Toledo (Ciudad Real) became a DO pago in 2006. Marcial Gómez Sequeira grows Cabernet Sauvignon, Merlot, and Syrah.

DO DOMINIO DE VALDEPUSA (PAGO)

This is the Marqués de Griñón's estate in the province of Toledo; one of the first to achieve pago status in 2003, growing Cabernet Sauvignon, Syrah, and Petit Verdot.

DO FINCA ELEZ (PAGO)

This was the other first pago DO, along with Valdepusa, founded by movie and theater director Manuel Manzaneque. His 3,281-foot high vineyards in the Sierra de Alcaraz (Albacete) grow Tempranillo, Cabernet Sauvignon, Merlot, and Chardonnay.

DO LA MANCHA

Europe's largest delimited quality-wine zone in Ciudad Real, Toledo, Cuenca, Albacete, and Guadalajara is back from the dead after years of neglect and now turning out some excellent-value wines from Cencibel, Syrah, and Merlot. A number of incremental DO areas have been created within it since 2001 (*see* below).

DO MANCHUELA

Another area bridging the gap between La Mancha, Valencia, and Murcia, it achieved DO status in 2000. The main grape is the Bobal (as in Valencia) for red wines. There has been a good deal of investment in new bodegas in recent years, including the single-estate Finca Sandoval, which belongs to Spanish celebrity wine-writer Victor de la Serna.

DO MENTRIDA

This is one of those forgotten areas of Spain, even though some of the biggest companies make wine here under the VdlT de Castilla (*see* right). There is potential, and land prices are low, even though it's only 44 miles from Madrid. There are 38 bodegas, of which 15 still don't bottle wine. Traditional reds are Tempranillo and Garnacha, but Cabernet Sauvignon, Merlot, Syrah, and Petit Verdot are making waves.

DO MONDEJAR

An area east of Madrid and north of La Mancha that still has to reach its potential, most of the wines are *jóvenes* for immediate drinking, made from Macabeo (white) and Tempranillo (red).

DO RIBERA DEL JUCAR

The first incremental DO to be lifted out of the La Mancha DO, in 2003. Bodegas can make wines under either name, according to the origin of the grapes. Production centers around the village of Pozoamargo, in the east of the province of Cuenca.

DO UCLES

This was the second incremental DO to be lifted out of La Mancha, in 2006. As with Ribera del Júcar, bodegas can make wine under either DO, according to the origin of the grapes. Uclés is the center of the area, in the province of Cuenca, southeast of Madrid.

DO VALDEPENAS

One of the early classics in Ciudad Real that really did make something of the Cencibel, traditionally oak-aged, warm, and mature, at silly prices. Some of Spain's best-value reds come from here.

OTHER WINES

VdlT de Castilla The first region-wide VdlT zone in Spain, created in 2000 to allow winemakers flexibility in the grapes they grow and the methods they use. Tempranillo, Cabernet Sauvignon, Merlot, and Syrah are the main varieties.

There are two other VdlT zones: Gálvez (Toledo), which makes everyday wines from Macabeo, Garnacha, Cencibel, and Cabernet Sauvignon; and Pozohondo (Albacete), which does the same, mainly with Monastrell and Airén.

Main Bodegas
(listed in alphabetical order), PRODUCER NAME; town/village; web/E-mail address; best wines (r = red, w = white)
A star (*) indicates particularly good quality.

DO ALMANSA
PIQUERAS; Almansa; www.bodegaspiqueras.es; Castillo de Almansa (r, w)

DO DEHESA DEL CARRIZAL (PAGO)
DEHESA DEL CARRIZAL; Retuerta del Bullaque; wwwdehesadelcarrizal.com; Dehesa del Carrizal (r, w)*

DO DOMINIO DE VALDEPUSA (PAGO)
DOMINIO DE VALDEPUSA; Malpica de Tajo; www.pagosdefamilia.com; Emeritus (r)*, Summa Varietalis (r)

DO FINCA ELEZ (PAGO)
FINCA ELEZ; El Bonillo; www.manuelmanzaneque.com; Manuel Manzaneque (r, w)*

DO LA MANCHA
www.lamanchado.es

ALEJANDRO FERNANDEZ; Campo de Criptana; www.elvinculo.com; El Vínculo (r)

FINCA ANTIGUA; Los Hinosos; www.fincaantigua.com; Finca Antigua (r), Clavis (r)*

MUNOZ; Noblejas; vibomu@teleline.es; Blas Muñoz (w)*

VINÍCOLA DE CASTILLA; Manzanares; www.vinicoladecastilla.com; Castillo de Alhambra (r, w), Señorío de Guadianeja (r)

DO MANCHUELA
www.do-manchuela.com

FINCA SANDOVAL; Ledaña; www.grandespagos.com/sandoval.html; Finca Sandoval (r)*

PONCE; Villanueva de la Jara; ponce@iniestahoy.com; Clos Lojen (r), P.f (r)

DO MENTRIDA
www.domentrida.es

FINCA LA VERDOSA; La Verdosa; www.arrayan.es; Arrayán Premium (r)*

DO MONDÉJAR
crdom@crdomondejar.com

MARISCAL; Mondéjar; www.mariscal.es; Cueva de los Judios (r), Tierra Rubio (r)

DO RIBERA DEL JUCAR
www.vinosriberadeljucar.com

CASA GUALDA; Pozoamargo; www.casagualda.com; Casagualda (r)

LA MAGDALENA; Casas de Haro; vmoragona@ucaman.es; Vega Moragona (r)

DO UCLES
www.vinosdeucles.com

URIBES MADERO; Huete; www.pagodecalzadilla.net; Calzadilla (r), Gran Calzadilla (r)*

DO VALDEPENAS
www.dovaldepenas.es

DIONISOS; Valdepeñas; www.agrobio-dionisos.com; Dionisos (r)

FELIX SOLIS; Valdepeñas; www.felixsolis.com; Viña Albali (r)

LOS LLANOS; Valdepeñas; www.gbvinartis.com; Pata Negra (r), Señorío de los Llanos (r)

MIGUEL CALATAYUD; Valdepeñas; www.vegaval.com; Vegaval Plata (r)

VdlT DE CASTILLA
ARESAN; Villarobledo; info@bodegasaresan.com; Aresan 9 Meses (r)*

CASA DE LA VINA; Alhambra; www.domecqbodegas.com; Albor (r), Casa de la Viña (r)*

CASTIBLANQUE; Campo de Criptana; www.bodegascastiblanque.com; Baldor (r)

PAGO DEL VICARIO; Ciudad Real; www.pagodelvicario.com; 50-50 (r), Monagós (r)

SANCHEZ MULITERNO; El Bonillo; www.sanchez-muliterno.com; Vega Guijoso (r), Magnificus (r)*

VALLEGARCIA; Retuerta del Bullaque; www.vallegarcia.com; Vallegarcia Viognier (w)*, Syrah (r)*

Cataluña (Catalonia) is a prosperous gastronomic powerhouse, rather like the Basque Country, and it was once part of a much larger empire which stretched, at its peak, as far as possessions in Greece and Turkey. Today it's a "nation within Spain" consisting of four provinces: Girona, Barcelona, Tarragona, and Lérida.

Cataluña is solidly Mediterranean in outlook, gastronomy, and wines, with a flourishing independent spirit evident in its art (Picasso, Dalí) and architecture (Gaudí, Puig i Cadafalch) and, indeed, every aspect of cultural life. The city of Barcelona with its grand *ramblas* (boulevards) and bustling lifestyle is one of the most exciting cities in the world, as well as being Spain's largest seaport.

Cataluña

LOCAL SPECIALTIES

Although seafood is the staple, particularly along the coast, Cataluña has a rich farming and produce heritage: beef from the high Pyrenees (*ternera de los Pirineos Catalanes*) and associated dairy products, including the specialty cheese *L'Alt Urgell y La Cerdanya*: mild and creamy, and also butter from the province of Lérida. Poultry and pork are also farmed, particularly in the province of Barcelona, with the *Pollo y Papón del Prat*—special breeds of chicken raised in Baix Llobregat—and *salchichón de Vic*, a spicy sausage from the Plana de Vic: only 28 villages are allowed to produce it. As with every other region, *jamón serrano* (cured ham) is ever-present.

Cataluña is a rich source of fruit and vegetables, with listings for *manzana* (apple) *de Girona*, *clementias* (clementines) *de las tierras del Ebro* (Tarragona), olives, citrus fruit, nuts (including the protected *avellana de Reus* (hazelnuts) in Tarragona), *patata de Prades* (potatoes from Tarragona), and rice, which is grown around the Ebro delta as it flows into the Mediterranean. There are four olive-oil areas: Les Garrigues (Lérida), Siurana, Terra Alta, and Baix Ebre Montsià (all in Tarragona). And the region as a whole is famous for its confectionery: *turrón* (nougat), chocolate bonbons, praline, and Catalan cookies known as *panellets* (sweet and savory) and *neules* (sweet). The *Generalitat de Catalunya* (Catalan government) also awards its own quality marks to various local products, including pork, rabbit, lamb, and honey.

They say in Cataluña that the purpose of eating together is to have a conversation: the food simply gives you something to do with your hands while you're talking. Nevertheless, a typical Catalan meal with seafood, fruit, vegetables, meat, olive oil, and wine is the very model of the healthy Mediterranean diet.

Catalan cooking is exciting and inspirational: its influence is felt throughout the Mediterranean. At times, the dishes are brilliantly simple. Take this colorful mixture of vegetables for example. The name comes from the verb *escalivar*, which literally means "to roast over hot ashes." Whole vegetables are roasted, then peeled, chopped, and artfully arranged as a "tart" to be served as an appetizer, or to accompany meat and fish.

Escalibada de verduras
Traditional roasted vegetables

INGREDIENTS (SERVES 4)

2 eggplants

3 red bell peppers

2 tomatoes

1 onion

1 whole garlic bulb

extra-virgin olive oil

Sherry vinegar (optional)

salt and freshly ground black pepper, to taste

fresh dill sprigs, to garnish

Preheat the oven to 350°F. Wash and dry the eggplants, peppers, and tomatoes and place in an ovenproof dish with the onion and garlic. Drizzle over some olive oil and sprinkle on a little salt. Roast in the oven for about 20 minutes until tender. (The onion requires the most cooking.) Remove the dish from the oven and set aside to cool.

When warm, peel the vegetables, tomatoes and garlic cloves. Cut the aubergines and peppers into fine strips, and the tomatoes and onion into segments. Keep all the vegetables separate from one another. Dress each with plenty of olive oil, and a few drops of sherry vinegar if desired, then set aside in the refrigerator to chill.

On a large, flat plate, assemble a round, vegetable "tart," about 8 inches in diameter. Arrange the strips of red pepper around the outside, and then, working inward, a ring of onion segments, eggplant strips, tomato wedges, and finish with a pile of soft garlic in the center. Cut it into 4 portions, and use a cake slice to transfer the slices to individual plates. Garnish each slice with a sprig of fresh dill.

WINE TIPS

SPECIAL OCCASION: **Venus, Venus la Universal, Montsant (€€€)**
SUNDAY LUNCH: **Raïmat Cabernet-Sauvignon, Costers del Segre (€€)**
EVERYDAY: **Tempranillo Clàssic, Albet i Noya, Penedès (€)**

The entire Spanish Mediterranean coast enjoys numerous variations of this dish. All contain rice, and are cooked in a *paellera* (paella pan). To many, the best part of the whole dish is the *socarrat*, the slightly burnt crust on the bottom of the pan. This version makes the most of the excellent seafood caught off the Catalan coast and boasts a sophisticated black color.

Socarrat de arroz negro con pulpitos

Pan-toasted black rice socarrat and baby octopus

INGREDIENTS (SERVES 4)

3 tablespoons olive oil

1 onion, finely chopped

1 green bell pepper, finely
    chopped

2 cups fish stock

2 garlic cloves, finely chopped

1 tomato, finely chopped

2oz angler fish

2oz hake

1oz mussels

2oz shrimp

1 cup short-grain rice (*calasparra* is
    the traditional paella rice, but
    arborio rice gives similar results)

2 bags squid ink

salt and pepper, to taste

2 bay leaves

1lb 2oz baby octopus

GARNISH

1 lemon, cut into 8 wedges

chopped fresh parsley

Heat the olive oil in a *paellera* or a very wide, flat skillet, and sauté the onion and pepper over a medium heat. Meanwhile, bring the fish stock to a boil and then set aside.

Add the garlic and tomato to the pan, stir for a few seconds, then add all the seafood, except for the baby octopus. Sauté until golden. Before adding the unwashed rice to the pan, measure its volume in a measuring jug. Then tip into the pan and continue to sauté. Pour in the ink and stir until the rice is well dyed.

Pour the hot fish stock into a measuring jug so that its volume is double the measured quantity of rice, and stir into the *paellera*. Flavor with salt, pepper, and the bay leaves, and allow to cook over a low heat for about 15 minutes, without stirring. Preheat the oven to 350°F. Put the *paellera* into the oven for 15 minutes until a crust forms.

Meanwhile, wash the baby octopus, and cook under a medium broiler for 5 minutes. Arrange the baby octopus evenly around the edge of the *paellera*. Garnish the top of the paella with lemon wedges and chopped parsley.

Place the *paellera* ceremoniously in the center of the table as a center piece. From there, serve individual portions, taking care to include a little of each ingredient, including the base—the *socarrat*—which should be crisp and toasted.

WINE TIPS

SPECIAL OCCASION: **Milmanda Chardonnay, Miguel Torres, Conca de Barberà (€€€)**
SUNDAY LUNCH: **Nerola Fermentado en Barrica, Miguel Torres, Catalunya (€€)**
EVERYDAY: **Marfil Pansà Blanca, Alella Vinícola Can Jonc, Alella (€)**

Once tasted, the exquisite flavor of *romescu* is never forgotten. Basically, it's a sauce of crushed dried bell peppers (from which it gets its name) and varying ingredients originated in Tarragona, and has transcended its coarse seafaring origins to accompany the most sophisticated recipes. Although the counterpoint to a good cod, in contrast with some pieces of bitter fruits, as proposed here, it is not easily beaten.

Bacalao confitado con romescu y dados de frutas ácidas

Salt cod with romescu sauce and fresh fruit

INGREDIENTS (SERVES 4)

FOR THE SALT COD

2lb 4oz salt cod fillets,
   with skin
olive oil
1 garlic bulb, cloves peeled but
   not chopped

FOR THE *ROMESCU* SAUCE

9oz onions
1lb 2oz tomatoes
1 garlic bulb
3 or 4 dried bell peppers, soaked
   for 2-3 hours to soften
1oz bread
15-20 almonds
1 cup olive oil
6 tablespoons wine vinegar
salt and black pepper, to taste

THE FRUIT

1 orange, peeled and segmented
1 kiwi fruit, peeled and sliced
2 slices of fresh pineapple

Put the salt cod in enough cold water to cover and soak in the refrigerator overnight. Try to change the water 2 or 3 times so that the fish releases as much salt as possible at a cool, constant temperature. Drain and dry the salt cod.

In a deep skillet, heat plenty of olive oil. When very hot, fry the whole garlic cloves until browned all over, then remove from the skillet and set aside. Reheat the olive oil and add the salt cod fillets to the skillet, skin-side down. The oil should cover the cod. Fry over a low heat for about 8 minutes until the cod is cooked, then remove from the pan and set aside. Save some of the olive oil to serve later.

Preheat the oven to 350°F. Rub all the solid ingredients for the *romescu* sauce with olive oil, including the dried peppers, and spread out on a baking sheet. Roast everything in the oven, remembering to remove each different ingredient when cooked. In particular, keep an eye on the almonds, bread, and dried peppers, which burn most easily.

When all the ingredients are roasted, remove from the oven and grind to a paste in a mortar and pestle. Press the paste through a sieve to remove any bits. Mix in the olive oil, vinegar, salt, and pepper.

Pour a tablespoon of the olive oil in which the salt cod was cooked onto each warmed plate. Place a piece of salt cod and a tablespoon of the *romescu* sauce next to the oil, with some fruit to one side. Pour the remaining sauce into a bowl and place on the table as an accompaniment.

WINE TIPS

SPECIAL OCCASION: **Closa Battlet Blanc, Ripoll Sins, Priorat (€€€)**
SUNDAY LUNCH: **Vía Edetana Crianza, Edetana, Terra Alta (€€)**
EVERYDAY: **Castell del Remei Blanc Planell, Costers del Segre (€)**

The profusion of fresh vegetables that the Catalans use in their cooking results in some spectacularly colorful and richly-flavored dishes. *Sanfaina*, a chunky ratatouille-type vegetable stew, is a typical example. It's amazing how such a simple local dish can transform a plate of smoked sardines into a culinary delight.

Crujientes de lomo de sardines ahumados con sanfaina guisada

Crunchy smoked sardines with mixed vegetables

INGREDIENTS (SERVES 4)

8 sardines

250g (9oz) smoked salt

1 unsliced loaf of bread

olive oil

1 onion

1 green bell pepper

1 red bell pepper

1 eggplant

1 zucchini

4 red tomatoes

salt and freshly ground black
    pepper, to taste

GARNISH

bunch of chives, chopped

sprig of marjoram

Clean the sardines, remove the bones, and separate the fillets.

Preheat the oven to 325°F. Cover the base of a large ovenproof dish with half the smoked salt and place the sardines on top, skin-side down. Cover with the remaining salt and put in the oven for 15 minutes. When the fish are cooked, remove from the salt and set aside.

Reduce the oven temperature to 300°F. Carefully cut the bread into very thin slices —it's easier to stand the loaf on end and cut the slices horizontally. Arrange the slices in a single layer on baking sheets. Drizzle over a little olive oil and bake in the oven for 10-15 minutes until crisp and golden.

Peel and chop the vegetables into largish pieces. Heat a drizzle of olive oil in a skillet and lightly sauté the vegetables and tomatoes over a medium heat until tender. Then season with salt and pepper.

Spoon the vegetables into the center of a serving dish, top with the crisp toast slices, and place the sardines over the toast. Garnish with chopped chives and a sprig of marjoram.

WINE TIPS

SPECIAL OCCASION: **Avgvstvs Chardonnay, Puig & Roca, Penedès (€€€)**
SUNDAY LUNCH: **Lanius, Alta Alella, Alella (€€)**
EVERYDAY: **Castillo Perelada Blanc de Blancs, Empordà-Costa Brava (€)**

Wines of Cataluña

Cataluña has eleven DO wine areas, and is also the heartland for Cava sparkling wine. Although Cava is made elsewhere in Spain, the Cava DO is dealt with here.

Catalan wine astonishes with its diversity. The three classic white-wine grapes are the Macabeo, Parellada, and Xarel-lo, and they're found in all kinds of combinations, especially in Cava, sometimes with an admixture of Chardonnay. The Catalan landscape offers excellent opportunities for vineyards, as the altitude climbs from 656 feet on the coast up to 2624 feet and more in the highlands. In general, everyday wines for the huge tourist industry are made from grapes grown at lower altitudes. The middle ground (984–1968 feet) is where more ambitious wines are made, and where many of the grapes for Cava are grown, as well as Tempranillo, Merlot, and Cabernet Sauvignon. The highest vineyards offer a cool-climate environment for the finest wines, and Pinot Noir, Sauvignon Blanc, and Chardonnay acquit themselves well. The result is a range of wines from world-class, structured reds and delicate, aromatic whites to everyday wines enjoyed in wholesale quantities in the beach-front resorts along the coast.

DO CATALUNYA

An (almost) region-wide classification created in 1999, which covers all existing DOs, giving their winemakers the opportunity to experiment, blend from different areas, and use grapes that might not be permitted in their home DOs. It also brought vineyards which were part of former VdlT areas into the DO system. Most producers are also members of other DOs.

DO ALELLA

Immediately north of Barcelona, this small area makes whites which are among Cataluña's best, made mainly from the three main varieties (*see above*) but also Chardonnay.

DO CONCA DE BARBERÀ

This region is gaining a reputation for everyday white wines made from the three Catalan classic varieties plus Chardonnay. Reds are from Cabernet Sauvignon and Merlot, and there is some Pinot Noir, Tempranillo, and Garnacha. The higher vineyards (up to 1,312 feet) produce excellent cool-climate wines.

DO COSTERS DEL SEGRE

In the province and around the city of Lleida (Lérida), this area has six subzones spread out rather like a clockface, some as far as 62 miles away. Ironically, the smallest of these, Raïmat, dominates the DO. It belongs to Cava giant Codorníu, and was the first to make serious, world-class wines here. Since the DO was established with just a few bodegas in 1987, there are now some two dozen at work.

DO EMPORDÀ-COSTA BRAVA

The northernmost DO in Cataluña. They're now making excellent whites from Sauvignon Blanc and Chardonnay, and reds from Tempranillo, Cabernet Sauvignon, and Merlot, alongside Garnacha and Cariñena; there's a good deal of experimentation with such as Syrah, Chenin Blanc, and even Riesling.

DO MONTSANT

Formerly part of the Tarragona DO. The vineyards are in the foothills of the Priorato DO, and the ambition is to make wines close to Priorato quality, but at affordable prices. There has been some considerable success capitalizing on old plantations of Garnacha and Cariñena.

DO PENEDÈS

The DO which put Cataluña on the map. The region has become one of Spain's best-known, not just for good-value wines but for some of the country's very finest. Many producers also make sparkling wines under the Cava DO.

DO PLA DE BAGES

Centred around Manresa, this ancient area grows the local Picapoll, Macabeo, and Parellada plus Chardonnay for whites, and Tempranillo, Garnacha, Pinot Noir, Cabernet Sauvignon, and Merlot for reds.

DOQ PRIORATO

This forgotten mountainside came back to life in the 1990s when visionary winemakers realized that grapes from abandoned ancient Garnacha and Cariñena vines could produce wonderfully characterful and concentrated wine. Since then, Cabernet Sauvignon, Merlot, and Syrah have been introduced, usually in minority amounts to lift the aromas of the old-vine wines. These are rare and low-yielding, and this is reflected in the price: there are no ordinary wines in Priorato.

DO TARRAGONA

Light, fresh everyday whites and reds, from Garnacha Blanca, Malvasía, Moscatel, and (recently) Chardonnay and Sauvignon Blanc. Reds include Garnacha, Tempranillo, and Cabernet Sauvignon. Some traditional sweet wines are still made (usually reds from Garnacha), and communion wine for the church is a major market

DO TERRA ALTA

Practically unheard-of ten years ago, this remote part of Tarragona is showing considerable promise, with new producers coaxing excellent wines out of Garnacha and Cariñena, with some help from Cabernet Sauvignon, Merlot, and Syrah.

DO CAVA

Cava is sparkling wine made by the traditional method, in the bottle, and also comes from other parts of Spain, but most are Catalan in origin, especially around the town of Sant Sadurní d'Anoia, in the province of Barcelona. Main grapes are the Catalan classics: Parellada, Macabeo, and Xarel-lo, but Chardonnay is also used, and some Pinot Noir for pink Cavas.

OTHER WINES/DRINKS

Parts of Cataluña still make the traditional *rancio*, which is allowed to oxidize in loosely stoppered bottles, often in the open air, until it turns brown or even black. Today the wines may be sweet or dry, but all have the characteristic, high-strength burnt flavor beloved of aficionados, and are generally served as a *digestivo*.

The other Catalan classic drink is *ratafía Catalana*, made by adding fresh grape juice to brandy so that the juice doesn't ferment and all the grape-sugars are preserved. Various versions are made, from simple, sweet, after-dinner wines to complex infusions usually aged in oak for three months or more.

Main Bodegas
(listed in alphabetical order), PRODUCER NAME; town/village; web/E-mail address; best wines (r = red, w = white)
A star (*) indicates particularly good quality.

DO CATALUNYA
www.do-catalunya.com

JEAN LEÓN; Torrelavid; www.jeanleon.com; Terrasola (rw)*

MIGUEL TORRES; Vilafranca del Penendès; www.torres.es; Nerola (rw)*

JOAN SARDÀ; Castellví de la Marca; www.joansarda.com; Feixes del Port (r)

DO ALELLA
www.doalella.com

ALELLA VINÍCOLA CAN JONC; Alella; www.alellavinicola.com; Ivori (w), Marfil (w)

PARXET; Tiana; www.parxet.es; Marqués de Alella (w)

ALTA ALELLA; Tiana; www.altaalella.com; Lanius (w)*, Dolç Mataró (sweet r)*

DO CONCA DE BARBERÀ
www.doconcadebarbera.com

ABADÍA DE POBLET; Poblet; www.grupocodorniu.com; Pinot Noir (r)*

CONCAVINS; Barberà de la Conca; www.bodegasconcavins.com; Clos Montblanc (r)

MIGUEL TORRES; Vilafranca del Penedès; www.torres.es; Milmanda (w)*, Grans Muralles (r)*

DO COSTERS DEL SEGRE
www.costersdelsegre.es

CASTELL DEL REMEI; Castell del Remei; www.castelldelremei.com; Gotim Bru (r)

CANTONELLA; La Pobla de Cérvoles; www.cervoles.com; Cérvoles (r)*

RAÏMAT Raïmat; www.raimat.com; Raïmat (rw)*

DO EMPORDÀ-COSTA BRAVA
doempcb@teleline.es

CASTILLO PERELADA; Perelada; www.castilloperelada.com; Gran Claustro (r)*, Ex Ex (r)*

PERE GUARDIOLA; Capmany; vins@pereguardiola.com; Floresta (p)*, Clos Foresta (r)

ESPELT; Vilajuiga; www.cellerespelt.com; Comabruna (r)*, Airam (sweet r)

DO MONTSANT
www.domontsant.com

CAPÇANES; Capçanes; www.cellercapcanes.com; Costers del Gravet (r), Cabrida (r)*

EUROPVIN FALSET; Falset; europvin@infonegocio.com; Laurona (r)*, 6 Vinyes de Laurona (r)*

VENUS LA UNIVERSAL; Falset; info@venuslauniversal.com; Dido (r), Venus (r)*

DO PENEDÈS
www.dopenedes.com

GRAMONA; Sant Sadurní d'Anoia; www.gramona.com; Gra a Gra (w)*, Mas Escorpi (w)*

JEAN LEÓN; Torrelavit; www.jeanleon.es; Vinya Gigi (w)*, Vinya Palau (r)

JOAN RAVENTÓS ROSELL; Masquefa; export@raventosrosell.com; Heretat Vall-Ventos (w)*, (r)

MIGUEL TORRES; Vilafranca del Penedès; www.torres.es; Mas la Plana (r)*, Reserva Real (r)*

PARÉS BALTÀ; Pacs del Penedès; www.paresbalta.com; Absis (r)*, Dominio Cusiné (r)*

RAVENTÓS I BLANC; Sant Sadurní d'Anoia; www.raventos.com; La Rosa (p)*, Isabel Negra (r)

DO PLA DE BAGES
www.dopladebages.com

GRAU Maians; www.vinsgrau.com; Jaume Grau Grau (rwp)

MASÍES D'AVINYÓ; Santa María d'Horta d'Avinyo; www.abadal.net; Abadal Chardonnay (w)*, Abadal Selecció (r)*

SOLERGIBERT; Artés; www.cellerssolergibert.com; Conxita Serra (r)*, Enric Solergibert Gran Selecció (r)*

DOQ PRIORATO
www.priorat.org

ÁLVARO PALACIOS; Gratallops; bodega@alvaropalacios.com; Finca Dofi (r)*, L'Ermita (r)*

CLOS FIGUERAS; Gratallops; europvin@infonegocio.com; Font de la Figuera (r)*, Clos Figueres (r)*

CLOS MOGADOR; Gratallops; closmogador@terra.es; Clos Mogador (r)*, Manyetes (r)*

COSTERS DEL SIURANA; Gratallops; www.costersdelsiurana.com; Clos de l'Obac (r)*, Miserere (r)*

SCALA DEI; Scala Dei; www.grupocodorniu.com; Cartoixa (r)*

VALL-LLACH; Porrera; www.vallllach.com; Embruix (r)*, Vall-Llach (r)*

DO TARRAGONA
dotarragona@ctmail.net

J.M. BACH I FILLS; Vila-Seca; www.closbarenys.com; Clos Barenys

DE MULLER; Reus; www.demuller.es; Chardonnay (w)*

DO TERRA ALTA
www.do-terraalta.com

ALTAVINS; Batea; www.altavins.com; Domus Pensi (r), Tempus (r)

BÀRBARA FORÉS; Gandesa; www.cellerbarbarafores.com; El Quinta (r), Coma d'En Pou (r)*

PIÑOL; Batea; www.vinospinol.com; L'Avi Arrufi (r)*, Mather Teresina (r)*

DO CAVA
www.crcava.es

AGUSTÍ TORELLÓ; Sant Sadurní d'Anoia; www.agustitorellomata.com; Kripta (w)*

ALSINA & SARDÀ; El Plà del Penedès; www.alsinasarda.com; Gran Reserva Especial (w)*, Brut (w)*

CODORNÍU; Sant Sadurní d'Anoia; www.grupocodorniu.com; Anna de Codorníu (w)*, Jaume de Codorníu (w)

FREIXENET; Sant Sadurní d'Anoia; www.freixenet.es; Reserva Real (w)*, Brut Barocco (w)*

GRAMONA; Sant Sadurní d'Anoia; www.gramona.com; Celler Batlle (w)*, Imperial (w)*

RAVENTÓS I BLANC; Sant Sadurní d'Anoía; www.raventos.com; l'Hereu (w)*, Manuel Raventós (w)

Extremadura is an agricultural cornucopia. If you can grow it, it grows here: cork, olives, tobacco, cotton, cereals—and vines, of course. In the livestock department, there are sheep, pigs, and goats, and it is rumored that the fabled spicy *chorizo* sausage and *jamón serrano* both have their origins in this pastoral landscape. Two of Spain's largest provinces, Cáceres in the north and Badajoz in the south reside here. The regional capital is the old Roman city of Mérida, although Badajoz has the largest population. Historically, this has been a relatively poor, sheep-herding area: indeed, they say that sheep still outnumber people in Extremadura.

Extremadura

LOCAL SPECIALTIES

Cheese is an important local product, and arguably Spain's finest cheese, *Torta del Casar*, comes from here. It's made from organic sheep milk, curdled with cardoon flowers, and salted before being matured into a round, cushion-shaped cheese, eaten by cutting a hole in the top and spooning out the contents. Other cheeses of note include *queso de la serena*, made in a similar fashion from the milk of Merino sheep, but often rather firmer when mature, and *queso ibores*, which is a harder, goat's milk cheese from Cáceres. Ham is the main classic from these parts, including the *pata negra* (black leg) cured hams known as *jamón Iberico*. The very best is *jamón Ibérico de bellota*, from free-range black pigs which have been fed on acorns in the three months prior to slaughter. *Ternera and cordero de Extremadura* (beef and lamb)are also available, from certified farmers and butchers.

Olive oil has its own *denominaciónes*, with specialty production in Monterrubio (Badajoz) of Cornezuelo and Picual olives, and Gata-Hurdes (Cáceres) with the Manzanilla Cacerena variety. Protected fruit and vegetables include the *cereza del Jerte*, cherries from the Jerte Valley in Cáceres, picked by hand and sized, graded, and certified by the *consejo regulador*, or regulating body. *Pimentón de la Vera* is the paprika from the Vera Valley in Cáceres. The peppers are smoked and dried after harvesting, and powdered before canning: they come sweet or hot according to taste.

There is a special honey made in Villuercas-Ibores (Cáceres) which comes in different styles, according to whether the pollen used in making it comes from flowers or the trees of the forest.

This is an archetypal Extremeña dish, uniting two great local delicacies on a single plate. The *solomillo* (pork tenderloin)—and *pata negra*, the region's cured ham—come from the semiwild black pigs which flourish in the cork-oak forests. *Torta del Casar* is arguably Spain's finest cheese. It's ripened until a lid can be cut in the crusty top and an almost liquid cheese spooned out.

Solomillo de cerdo Ibérico con binomio de queso de torta del casar y verduras escabechadas

Black-pig pork tenderloin with a duo of Torta del Casar and vegetables

INGREDIENTS (SERVES 4)

2 cups red wine

2 cups white wine

4 garlic cloves, peeled

freshly ground black pepper

1lb 12oz pork tenderloin

10oz *Torta del Casar*, or ripe brie, rind removed

4oz carrots

4oz zucchini

4oz celery

4oz eggplant

4oz scallions

1 leek

1 cup olive oil

2 teaspoons vinegar

1 teaspoon salt

1¹/₂oz mushrooms

1/3 cup red currants

1 teaspoon olive oil

1 teaspoon Sherry vinegar

handful of alfalfa sprouts, to garnish

Pour the red and white wines into a large bowl. Add the garlic, black pepper, and pork and marinate in the refrigerator for at least 24 hours.

Preheat the oven to 325°F and line a baking sheet with parchment paper. Spoon the cheese onto the sheet and bake for 5 minutes to form a thin crisp. Remove from the oven and set aside to cool.

Cut the carrots, zucchini, celery, eggplant, and scallions into sticks of equal length. Heat 1 tablespoon of olive oil in a skillet over a medium heat and sauté each vegetable separately until slightly softened but still crunchy. Cut the leek lengthwise into thin strips, and blanch for 30 seconds in boiling water until pliable. Put the vegetables into 4 separate bundles and tie together with a strand of leek. In a skillet, warm the olive oil, vinegar, and salt over a low heat for 2 minutes. Set aside to cool, then immerse the vegetable bundles in the salty oil to marinate.

Finely chop the mushrooms and put in a bowl with the red currants. Toss with 1 teaspoon of olive oil and 1 teaspoon of Sherry vinegar.

Remove the pork tenderloins from the marinade, pat dry, and place under a hot broiler for 10 minutes, turning, until well browned all over. Preheat the oven to 225°F. Transfer the pork tenderloins to a roasting pan and roast in the oven for 8 minutes, or until cooked through. While still warm, cut the pork into 4 pieces, each about 1½ inches long.

Place a piece of pork and a vegetable parcel on the plate, spoon a little red currant and mushroom salsa onto the side, and pour some of the salsa sauce around the base. Garnish with a wafer of crunchy cheese crisp and a handful of alfalfa sprouts.

WINE TIPS

SPECIAL OCCASION: **Tallant de Vega Esteban, Ventura de Vega, Ribera del Guadiana (€€€)**
SUNDAY LUNCH: **Puerta Palma Finca Las Tenderas, Marcelino Díaz, Ribera del Guadiana (€€)**
EVERYDAY: **Celtus, Viña Santa Marina, Extremadura (€)**

In many of the poorer parts of Spain, necessity has always been the mother of invention. For generations, peasants have used their imaginations to create some ingenious, nourishing dishes from the most basic ingredients. In this instance, a tasty but humble dish of egg and onion fritters is elevated to fine-dining status when served with an extravagant sweet wine sauce.

Repápalos extremeños

Egg and onion fritters with tempura vegetables and a port and red-wine sauce

INGREDIENTS (SERVES 4)

6 eggs, beaten

2 garlic cloves, finely chopped

1 tablespoon chopped fresh parsley

1 teaspoon chopped fresh thyme

salt and pepper, to taste

4 thick slices day-old white bread, crusts removed, reduced to crumbs in a food processor

1 onion, finely chopped

6 tablespoons olive oil

7oz duck's liver

1 cup port

1 cup red wine

1 cup Pedro Ximénez dessert wine

1 cup water

2 teaspoons ground black pepper

2 bay leaves

1 tablespoon superfine sugar

FOR THE GARNISH

1/4 cup all-purpose flour

16 spinach or Swiss chard leaves

Mix the eggs, garlic, parsley, thyme, salt, pepper, bread crumbs, and half the onion together vigorously to form a stiff paste.

Heat 2 tablespoons of the olive oil in a skillet and sauté the rest of the onion until softened. Puree the liver and onion with a drizzle of port, red wine, and Pedro Ximénez in a food processor. Season with salt and pepper. Divide the bread paste into 12 equal pieces and rub each between your palms to shape a medium-size ball. Poke a finger into each ball and hide a small quantity of liver puree in the center. Seal up the hole by pinching the sides together and carefully reshaping the ball.

Pour the remaining port and wine, water, pepper, and bay leaves into a saucepan and bring to a boil over a medium heat. Then drop in the bread balls and poach for 10 minutes until slightly puffed-up and firm. Drain well on paper towels. Then heat the remaining olive oil in a skillet over a medium heat, add the bread balls, and fry, turning frequently, until golden. Drain on paper towels.

Bring the port and wine back to a boil, and simmer until thickened to a sauce consistency. Meanwhile, pour the rest of the Pedro Ximénez into a skillet, stir in the sugar, and boil to reduce until syrupy.

Beat the flour with a little ice water to make a light tempura batter. Dip the spinach in the batter so the leaves are only lightly coated. Fry in hot oil until crisp.

Pour 3 pools of port and wine sauce onto each plate. Place a fritter on top of each. Garnish with spinach or Swiss chard leaves and a drizzle of the Pedro Ximénez sauce around the plates.

WINE TIPS

SPECIAL OCCASION: **Corte Real Platinum, Extremeña, Extremadura (€€€)**

SUNDAY LUNCH: **Dominium Merlot, Medina Hermosos, Extremadura (€€)**

EVERYDAY: **Torremayor, Santa Marina, Ribera del Guadiana (€)**

Retinto is a breed of cattle, the finest of Spain's indigenous breeds. They are reared on the lush pastures of Extremadura and Andalucía, and allowed to roam freely over the green grass throughout their lives. The cattle are sent to slaughter when they are about 12 months old. Such special treatment ensures that their meat has a superior flavor, tenderness, and succulence, which clearly distinguishes it from all other beef.

Caldereta de añojo retinto con Amanita cesárea confitada, vainilla y flor de huevo

Tender beef casserole with wild mushrooms, sweetened with vanilla

INGREDIENTS (SERVES 4)

4 tablespoons olive oil

2lb *retinto*, or other
    tender beef, cut into cubes

salt and pepper, to taste

5 garlic cloves, chopped

7oz carrots, cut into sticks

4 leeks, finely sliced

14oz onions, chopped

4 bay leaves and 2 sprigs of thyme

choricero peppers, ground

1/4 cup flour

2 cups red wine

1 cup beef stock or water

4oz wild mushrooms

1 vanilla bean

1 green bell pepper, finely chopped

1 red bell pepper, finely chopped

1/2 eggplant, finely chopped

1/2 zucchini, finely chopped

1 cup Sherry vinegar

GARNISH

2 cups Pedro Ximénez wine

4 eggs (optional)

Heat half the olive oil in a flameproof casserole over a medium heat. Season the beef with salt and pepper, then fry in batches, until browned all over. When the last batch is browned, return all the beef to the casserole and add the garlic, carrots, 2 of the leeks, onions, bay leaves, thyme, and *choricero*. Sauté until the onions start browning, then stir in the flour with a wooden spoon and pour in the red wine. Bring to a boil and allow to thicken before stirring in the stock. Simmer over a medium heat for about 1 hour, until the meat is tender and cooked through. Transfer the meat to a saucepan. Strain the sauce through a sieve over the meat. and set aside to reheat before serving.

Meanwhile, preheat the oven to 225°F. Spread the mushrooms on a baking sheet and drizzle over a little olive oil. Split the vanilla bean, scrape out the seeds and sprinkle onto the mushrooms, cook in the oven for 6 minutes.

In a skillet, heat the remaining olive oil. Sauté the green and red peppers, eggplant, and zucchini briefly before pouring in the Sherry vinegar. Continue cooking over a medium heat for about 10 minutes until browned.

Reduce the Pedro Ximénez in a saucepan until syrupy and glossy.

In a skillet, fry small batches of the remaining leeks in olive oil until crunchy. Drain on paper towels.

Spoon some meat with the sauce into the center of each plate, and place some sautéed vegetables and mushrooms alongside. Garnish with a crown of fried leeks and a drizzle of Pedro Ximénez around the edge of the plate. Top everything off with a poached egg, if desired.

WINE TIPS

SPECIAL OCCASION: **Tallant de Vega Esteban, Ventura de Vega, Ribera del Guadiana (€€€)**
SUNDAY LUNCH: **Puerta Palma Finca Las Tenderas, Marcelino Díaz, Ribera del Guadiana (€€)**
EVERYDAY: **Celtus, Viña Santa Marina, Extremadura (€)**

The wild birds and small game that inhabit the beautiful Extremaduran countryside have always played an important part in the local diet. Fresh herbs and marinades are widely used to flavor and tenderize the meat: here, sprigs of fresh rosemary infuse the rabbit with a sweet scent of grassy fields. The asparagus and fruit add a modern flourish to the taste of the dish.

Conejo al romero
Rabbit with fresh rosemary

INGREDIENTS (SERVES 4)

1 rabbit
salt and freshly ground black
    pepper, to taste
1 cup fresh rosemary
1 cup extra-virgin olive oil
1/2 cup superfine sugar
2 teaspoons water

FOR THE SAUCE

2 tablespoons superfine sugar
2/3 cup water
1/3 cup blueberries
3/4 cup port
3/4 cup red wine
2 drops rosemary extract
2 cups beef stock

GARNISH

12 asparagus spears, trimmed
3 Golden Delicious apples, peeled
    and cut into sticks
1/2 cup red currants
4 sprigs fresh rosemary

Once the rabbit is clean, remove the head and cut cleanly through the rib cage midway between the fore and hind legs. Then split the joints in half lengthwise, and separate into 4 pieces, each with a leg and part of the saddle. Then bone out the saddle part. Make a hole in the center of each saddle flap, and push the leg through up to the thigh. Tie the bone and meat together with cooking string.

Preheat the oven to 225°F. Make a straight cut in the lower part of the thigh visible below the flap. Rub salt and pepper, and rosemary into the cut. Then rub olive oil all over the legs, place in a roasting pan and roast in the oven for 10 minutes. Then broil the legs until golden brown.

Meanwhile, put the sugar and water into a casserole and heat gently to form a light caramel. Add the fried rabbit to the casserole, cover, and cook gently for 45 minutes.

For the sauce, put the sugar and water into a saucepan, bring to a boil over a medium heat, stirring until the sugar is dissolved. Continue boiling to form a light caramel. Then caramelize the blueberries over a low heat for about 15 minutes. Allow to cool, then blend in a food processor, and strain the puree through a sieve. Pour the port, wine, and 2 drops of rosemary extract into a saucepan, bring to a boil over a medium heat and simmer to reduce by half. Add the beef stock, return to a boil, and continue to reduce over a low heat for another 15 minutes.

For the garnish, cook the asparagus in boiling water for 5 minutes. Arrange with the apple on a baking sheet. Brush with olive oil and place under a hot broiler to brown. Spoon a trail of the sauce down the center of each plate. Place a portion of rabbit on top. To one side, place 2 sticks of apple and prop up 3 asparagus tips against them. Add a flourish of port and wine sauce and garnish with red currants, and rosemary.

WINE TIPS

SPECIAL OCCASION: **Puerta Palma Finca El Campillo, Marcelino Díaz, Ribera del Guadiana (€€€)**
SUNDAY LUNCH: **Attelea Crianza, Ruiz Torres, Ribera del Guadiana (€€)**
EVERYDAY: **Privilegio de Romale, Antonio Ortiz Ciprián, Ribera del Guadiana (€)**

Wines of Extremadura

There's only one DO wine in Extremadura: Ribera del Guadiana, named after the vineyards along the valley of the River Guadiana which flows through Badajoz and, for some of its course, forms the border between Spain and Portugal before flowing into the Atlantic in the Gulf of Cádiz. This is a relatively new DO, created in 1997 from six country-wine areas which had been chipping away at the international market for many years. They became subzones of the DO, still keeping their original names, which may be mentioned on the label: Montánchez (central Cáceres), Cañamero (southeastern Cáceres), Ribera Baja del Guadiana (western Badajoz), Ribera Alta del Guadiana (eastern Badajoz), and Tierra de Barros (central and southeastern Badajoz). This last is centered on Almendralejo, and one bodega in particular, Inviosa (now Bodegas Lar de Barros), first cracked the export market to let the world know that Extremadura could make wines at this level. Managing Director Marcelino Díaz created a new boutique bodega to drive the point home.

A wide variety of grapes are grown, including the local Cayetana, Pardina, Borba, Chelva, and Montúa for whites, and Garnacha Tintorera and Jaén Tinto for reds. Most wines of export quality will be made mainly from Tempranillo, Cabernet Sauvignon, Graciano, Mazuela, Merlot, Monastrell, Syrah, and even a little Pinot Noir.

VdlT EXTREMADURA

Some producers didn't want to join the DO in 1997, and outside investors were attracted by the quality (and low price) of land in Extremadura, so the local government created the *vino de la tierra* (VdlT) to allow flexibility and a free hand and to encourage inward investment. There are now around eight bodegas working within the VdlT, five of whom are also members of the DO. Tempranillo, Cabernet Sauvignon, and Garnacha are the favored grapes for the (mainly) red wines.

Main Bodegas

(listed in alphabetical order), PRODUCER NAME; town/village; web/E-mail address; best wines (r = red, w = white)
A star (*) indicates particularly good quality.

DO RIBERA DEL GUADIANA
www.riberadelguadiana.org

LAR DE BARROS; Almendralejo; www.lardebarros.com; Lar de Lares (r), Lar de Oro (r)

MARCELINO DÍAZ; Alendralejo; www.madiaz.com; Puerta Palma Finca El Campillo (r)*, Finca Las Tenderas (r)

DOLORES MORENAS; Los Santos de Maimona; www.doloresmorenas.com; Melithon (r), Real Provisión (r)

VdlT EXTREMADURA
LUÍS GURPEGUI MUGA; San Adrian (Navarra); www.gurpegui.es; Gurpegui (r), Pintoresco (r)

MEDINA HERMOSO; Medina de la Torres; www.medina.cc; Dominium (r)

This is a beautiful area north of Portugal known as "Green Spain" for the lushness of its vegetation and its Atlantic weather influences: cool by Spanish standards with magnificent river valleys with steep, craggy banks and almost fjord-like estuaries (*rías*) in the north (*rías altas*) and west (*rías baixas*). The capital is Santiago de Compostela, whose cathedral has been a pilgrimage destination for more than 1,000 years. Galicia's origins are Celtic and Celtic imagery is to be found everywhere.

Galicia has four provinces: A Coruña and Pontevedra along the west coast, and Lugo and Ourense inland. A Coruña is the port from which the Spanish Armada sailed against England in 1588, and still has a strong maritime tradition.

Galicia

LOCAL SPECIALTIES

Queso tetilla is a cow's-milk cheese, originally from the A Coruña/Pontevedra border, although it is now made throughout the region. *Cebreiro* (cow's milk with a maximum of 40 percent goat's milk), *San Simón da Costa* (Alpine and Frisian cow's milk), and *arzúa-ulloa* (cow's milk) are all cheeses made in A Coruña and Lugo.

Seafood is the most prevalent dish in every restaurant, although the torrential rivers gushing forth from the coastal crags are breeding-grounds for *lampreas* (lampreys). Other waterborne food includes crab, lobster, crayfish, sea bass, turbot. *Pulpo á la Gallega* (octopus with olive oil and sweet paprika) is widely regarded as the best octopus in Spain; *centollo*, or spiny crab, is another local specialty. The signature dish of the region is, however, *percebes* (goose foot barnacles). An edible member of the barnacle family, they're usually served as a starter with a strong pair of pliers to get them open, with the local Albariño wine. *Mejillones de Galicia* (mussels from the rías) also have their own *denominación*. *Ternera Gallega* is the protected name of meat from the local cattle, and the local cured ham, known as *lacón Galego*, has its own DO.

Patata de Galicia is the *denominación* for potatoes of the Kennebec variety grown in specific areas; another local vegetable is *grelo*, a kind of slightly bitter, spinach-like vegetable sometimes described as turnip tops, and unique to this part of Spain.

The small village of Cea in Orense produces *pan de Cea*, a bread produced there since medieval times in domed, granite, wood-burning ovens. Finally, *miel de Galicia*, the local honey, comes in various exotic styles, is tightly protected, and named according to its delicate nuances: *milflores* (floral), *eucalypto* (eucalyptus), *castaño* (chestnut), and *silva* (woodland).

In Galicia, they eat all manner of seafood and fish, from barnacles and squid to turbot and horse mackerel. Also known as scad, the horse mackerel is one of most popular blue fish in Spain. In this stew, its intense flavor is more than a match for the wine and pepper. Together they represent the essence of the Gallego diet.

Caldero de jurel encebollado con chipirón de anzuelo y caldo corto especiado

Spicy horse-mackerel stew with onion and baby squid

INGREDIENTS (SERVES 4)

FOR THE SPICY FISH STOCK
7oz fish heads and bones
1 leek, sliced
1 carrot, sliced
1 onion, quartered
ground pepper
6 tablespoons fruity white wine
1 tablespoon cider vinegar

FOR THE STEW
3 potatoes, peeled and diced
4 medium horse mackerel steaks
salt and pepper
2 tablespoons olive oil
2 onions, sliced
1lb 2oz baby squid
1 bay leaf

FOR THE SALSA
2 tablespoons olive oil
5 garlic cloves, peeled and crushed
pinch of ground white pepper
1 tablespoon vinegar
1 teaspoon paprika

To make the stock, put all the fish stock ingredients in a large saucepan with 4 cups cold water, bring to a boil over a high heat, then reduce the heat to low and simmer for 20 minutes. From time to time, skim off any residue that rises to the surface of the stock.

Strain the stock into another saucepan, add the potatoes and boil gently for about 15 minutes, until nearly cooked. Then season the horse mackerel with salt and pepper. Add to the saucepan and cook for an additional 10 minutes. Transfer the potatoes and horse mackerel to a bowl, and set the stock aside.

To make the salsa, heat the olive oil in a skillet over a low heat. Add the garlic and sauté until golden. Remove from the heat, let the cloves cool a little, then stir in the pepper, vinegar, and paprika. Set aside.

To assemble the fish stew, heat the olive oil in a casserole over a low heat, and sweat the onion for 5 minutes until softened. Then raise the heat to medium and sauté the baby squid with the onion. When the squid are cooked, add the potatoes, horse mackerel, most of the reserved stock, bay leaf, and salsa to the casserole, stirring so that the potatoes break down to thicken the sauce slightly. Simmer over a low heat for 3-4 minutes to let the flavors combine.

Serve a ladleful of the stew in each bowl, garnished with a few pieces of horse mackerel and a bay leaf (optional).

WINE TIPS

SPECIAL OCCASION: **Arautiam, Mar de Frades, Rías Baixas (€€€)**
SUNDAY LUNCH: **Terra Firme, Terra de Cruces, Rías Baixas (€€)**
EVERYDAY: **Pazo de Monterrey, Nuevo Milenio, Monterrei (€)**

No aficionado of northern Spanish cooking could resist the exquisite *empanadas* (pasty-like pies) that are the mainstay of Galician tapas. Corn flour, either on its own or mixed with wheat flour, is used for making the pastry, which gives the pies their golden color and tasty flavor. The *empanadas* are filled with the excellent fresh fish and shellfish that are caught off the coast all year round.

Empanada de sardinas asadas y verduras

Sardine, tomato, and red pepper pie

INGREDIENTS (SERVES 4)

FOR THE DOUGH

3¹/₂ cups wheat flour

3¹/₂ cups corn flour

pinch of salt

1 envelope active dry yeast

¹/₂ cup lard, at room temperature

2 cups lukewarm water

1 egg, beaten

FOR THE FILLING

2 red bell peppers

1 cup olive oil

3 onions, finely chopped

14oz tomatoes, peeled, seeded, and chopped

pinch of salt

1 bay leaf

2lb 4oz fresh sardines, cleaned, guts, heads, and scales removed

1 egg, beaten

Sift the flours onto a clean work surface and stir in the salt and yeast. Push the dry ingredients into a heap and make a well in the center. Put the lard, half the lukewarm water, and the egg into the well and mix together, adding more water as required and kneading vigorously to produce a smooth dough. Transfer to an oiled bowl, cover with a damp cloth, and leave in a warm place for about 1 hour to rise.

Preheat the oven to 350°F. Rub the peppers with a little olive oil and roast for 25 minutes. When cool, peel and cut the peppers into strips. Then heat 2 tablespoons of the olive oil in a skillet and sauté the onions over a medium heat for 5 minutes until softened but not browned. Add the pepper strips, tomatoes, salt, and bay leaf, and simmer for about 10 minutes until thickened.

Meanwhile, remove the bones from the sardines and separate the fillets.

Preheat the oven to 425°F. Cut the dough in two, making one piece slightly larger than the other. Sprinkle a little flour over the work surface and roll out the larger piece with a rolling pin. Brush olive oil around the inside of a large ovenproof dish and line with the dough, with a little spilling over the top all the way round. Spread half the pepper and tomato sauce onto the dough, arrange the sardines evenly on top, and then spread over the remaining sauce.

Roll out the rest of the dough and lay it over the top of the *empanada*, moistening and sealing the edges with your fingers. Trim to neaten. Prick the surface with a fork and make a small hole in the center for the steam to escape. Brush the top with beaten egg, and bake in the oven for about 40 minutes, until well browned.

Serve the *empanada*, either warm or cold, cut into squares.

WINE TIPS

SPECIAL OCCASION: **Pazo de Señorans Selección de Añada, Rías Baixas (€€€)**

SUNDAY LUNCH: **Valdesil Godello, Valderroa, Valdeorras (€€)**

EVERYDAY: **Gran Reboreda, Campante, Ribeiro (€)**

Galicia is the world's second-largest producer of mussels (after China) so, not surprisingly, mussels are the region's most popular fast-food. This recipe, serving mussels with octopus and potatoes, is a tribute to the familiar, deep-rooted flavors of the area. The local potatoes are called *cachelos*, and take their name from the *cachos* (small pieces) they are cut into for cooking.

Ravioli de pulpo con cachelo confitado en pimentón dulce sobre charlota de mejillón

Ravioli of octopus with confit potatoes in sweet paprika on a mussel cake

INGREDIENTS (SERVES 4)

6 tablespoons olive oil

1 teaspoon paprika or Spanish pimentón

2 *cachelos* (large potatoes), peeled, sliced thinly, and cut into 1/2-inch-wide strips

salt, to taste

1 octopus

1/2 red bell pepper, finely diced

1/2 green bell pepper, finely diced

1/2 onion, finely diced

2 gherkins, finely diced

1 tablespoon Sherry vinegar

1 tablespoon olive oil

salt and pepper, to taste

3/4 cup dry white wine

24 mussels, washed and debearded

1/2 cup agar agar

GARNISH

olive oil

seaweed, deep-fried (optional)

Heat the olive oil in a skillet and mix the paprika into the hot olive oil with a wooden spoon. Remove from the heat and allow to marinate for a few minutes. Then fry the potatoes in the paprika oil. When cooked and well browned, remove from the skillet, sprinkle with a little salt, and set aside.

Freeze the octopus tentacles. When well chilled and firm, carefully cut into slices. Lay 2 strips of potato to form a cross. In the center, place a slice of octopus. Wrap the potato around the octopus to make a ravioli-like parcel. Preheat the oven to 350°F. Brush a baking sheet with olive oil, arrange the potato raviolis on the sheet and place in the oven for about 10 minutes until the octopus is tender and the potato golden.

Mix the peppers, onion, and gherkins together, then add the vinegar, olive oil, and salt to make a salsa.

Tip the wine and mussels into a casserole, cover, and cook over a high heat for about 4 minutes until all the shells have opened. Discard any that don't. Remove the mussels from their shells. Pour 3/4 cup of the mussel stock into a saucepan and reduce on the stove for 30 minutes. Sprinkle in the agar agar and stir to dissolve and form a jelly. Allow to cool before stirring in most of the salsa (reserving some for a garnish). Set aside.

Line 4 small individual semicircular molds with the the mussels. Fill with a small portion of the salsa and cover the top with mussels. Put in the refrigerator until set. Carefully remove the mussel cakes from their molds. Place one on each plate, accompanied by some octopus "ravioli." Garnish with the remaining salsa, a few drops of olive oil, and fried seaweed, if desired.

WINE TIPS

SPECIAL OCCASION: **Don Pedro de Soutomaior Neve Carbónica, Galegas, Rías Baixas (€€€)**

SUNDAY LUNCH: **Airón, Alemparte, Ribeiro (€€)**

EVERYDAY: **Viña Godeval, Valdeorras (€)**

This nutritious dish is traditionally made in a three-legged iron *pote* (pot) hanging over an open fire, which is where it gets its name. It belongs to the family of hearty winter stews, which are so characteristic of the Spanish diet. What differentiates this Galician version from those of other regions is that this recipe always includes white beans, potatoes, and pork.

Pote Gallego
Traditional stew, Galicia-style

INGREDIENTS (SERVES 4)

3 cups dried chickpeas

1/2 cup navy beans

7oz stewing lamb

6oz salt pork

4 pieces of pig's ear

4oz ham

9oz *chorizo* sausages, chopped, plus extra to garnish

4 handfuls of turnip tops, or other green leaves, washed and shredded

1 *hueso de caña* (leg bone of beef)

salt, to taste

1 tablespoon olive oil

13/4 pint beef stock

10oz potatoes, peeled

fresh parsley, finely chopped, to garnish

The day before making this dish, put the chickpeas and beans into a large saucepan, cover with warm water and set aside to soak overnight. Also put the lamb, salt pork, pig's ear, ham, and *chorizos* in a saucepan, cover with cold water, and set aside to soak for 24 hours.

In a saucepan of boiling water, blanch the turnip tops with the leg bone, salt, and olive oil over a medium heat for 10 minutes, or until tender. When tender, remove from the heat, drain, cool under running cold water, and set aside.

In another large saucepan, place the lamb, salt pork, pig's ear, ham, and *chorizos*, cover with water, bring to a boil over a high heat, then turn the heat down and simmer over a low heat for 3 hours.

Drain the chickpeas and beans, and put in a cloth bag. In a separate saucepan, cook the chickpeas and beans in some meat stock for at least 1 hour until tender.

When the meats are nearly cooked, add the whole potatoes and the turnip tops. Continue to cook for about another 30 minutes over a low heat, until the potatoes are cooked and the meats are cooked through.

Serve the stew in deep bowls. Garnish with a few pieces of *chorizo* and a sprinkling of fresh parsley. Alternatively, serve the meats separately from the chickpeas and beans.

WINE TIPS

SPECIAL OCCASION: VX2 Cuvée Caco, María Álvarez Serrano, Ribeiro (€€€)
SUNDAY LUNCH: Thémara, Enológica Temera, Ribeira Sacra (€€)
EVERYDAY: Terra do Gargalo Tinto, Gargalo, Monterrei (€)

Wines of Galicia

Galicia has five DO zones and most of the best wines are white to match the local seafood. The most important grape is Albariño and it was this, particularly from the coastal Rías Baixas DO, that first brought fame to the region: the style is crisp, with fresh, peachy fruit and a delicious, lip-smacking finish. On the vine it has strong similarities to the Riesling: legend says that it was originally brought to Galicia by German monks on the pilgrimage trail to Santiago. Godello is the region's second grape: another fresh and crisp white, but with a gentle hint of hazelnuts on the finish. Many Galician wines also have some Treixadura and Loureira, which flourish in the more humid, inland valleys.

Although the red Mencía grape is grown all over the region, Galicia's only serious red wines come from the Ribeira Sacra DO. This is perhaps the most spectacularly beautiful part of the region, and the wines tend to be made by small producers. The style is light, with a smoky perfume and crisp fruit, often aided by a little oak. These wines are enjoyed young and fresh.

DO RIBEIRO

The oldest and biggest area, a continuation inland of Rías Baixas but in Ourense. Here Godello is the chief grape for white wine: lovely fruit but often with a delicious hazelnut finish.

DO VALDEORRAS

The furthest inland. Expect light, fruity reds from Mencía and delicate whites from Godello.

DO RIAS BAIXAS

Mainly along the western coast and the border with Portugal in Pontevedra, but there are some vineyards over the border in A Coruña. The Albariño grape is king here, making lovely, peachy-fruit whites with delicious acidity.

DO RIBERA SACRA

Mainly red wines made from Mencía along this beautiful valley in Ourense, which is dotted with ancient monasteries.

The wines range from delicious fruity gluggers to some seriously interesting stuff.

DO MONTERREI

The smallest of all, this is a mainly white-wine area growing Treixadura, Doña Blanca, and Godello. Reds are light and made mainly from Mencía and Bastardo.

OTHER WINES

VdIT Betanzos Light, everyday wines, reds from Alicante and Mencía, whites from Palomino and Albariño in the province of A Coruña.

VdIT Val do Miño-Ourense Another area for lightweight, everyday wines: whites from Albariño and Godello, reds from Mencía and Caiño.

OTHER DRINKS

Orujo (www.orujodegalicia.org) is Galicia's "national" drink. It's a clear spirit distilled from the pomace (grape skins), after the wine has been pressed (as with *marc* in France and *grappa* in Italy), and for some reason the grape-varieties grown in Galicia make a particularly smooth and fragrant spirit, albeit with the bite that comes with any *aguardiente* (*eau de vie*). Galegos drink it as a *digestivo* after a meal, most wineries produce it, and all restaurants stock it. As well as the basic spirit, it's available flavored with herbs and coffee.

One popular way of enjoying it is the *quemada* (literally "burned"): *orujo* is poured into a large earthenware bowl with sugar (½ cup for every 4 cups of spirit), orange and lemon peel, and coffee beans. Some enthusiasts also add other botanicals, and these are stirred in to steep in the liquid. The mixture is then ignited, and stirred using a long-handled ladle. Sometimes sugar is burnt in the ladle and poured in periodically during the stirring. The heat drives the flavors of the botanicals into the spirit and when the flames on the surface turn blue it's ready to drink—after a short period of cooling. The tradition goes back to the 11th century, and the elixir was once believed to have medicinal and even magical properties.

Main Bodegas
(listed in alphabetical order), PRODUCER NAME; town/village; web/E-mail address; best wines (r = red, w = white)
A star (*) indicates particularly good quality.

DO RIBEIRO
www.do-ribeiro.com

MARÍA ÁLVAREZ SERRANO; Leiro; www.cotodegomariz.com; Coto de Gomariz (w)*, VX2 Cuvée Caco (r)*

VIÑA MEÍN; Leiro; www.vinamein.com; Viña Meín (w)*, Viña Meín Tinto Clásico (r)

DO VALDEORRAS
www.dovaldeorras.com

DÍA-NOITE; Petín; www.galiciano.com; Galiciano Día (w), Galiciano Noite (r)

SANTA MARTA; Córgovo; santa.marta@teleline.es; Viñaredo Godello (w)*, Viñaredo Mencía (r)

DO RÍAS BAIXAS
www.doriasbaixas.com

AGNUS DEI; Meaño; www.vinumterrae.com; Agnus Dei (w)*

CASTRO MARTÍN; Puxafeita; www.bodegascastromartin.com; Castro Martin (w)*, Avián (w)*, Casal Caeiro (w)*

MARTÍN CÓDAX; Vilariño-Cambados; www.martincodax.com; Organistrum (w)*, Gallaecia (w)*, Martín Códax (w)*

DO RIBEIRA SACRA
www.ribeirasacra.org

MOURE; Saviñao; www.adegasmoure.com; Abadía da Cova (r)*, Abadía da Cova (w)*

RECTORAL DE AMANDI; Amandi; www.bodegasgallegas.com; Rectoral de Amandi (r)

DO MONTERREI
www.crdomonterrei.com

GARGALO; Verín; www.verino.es; Terra do Gargalo (w)*, Terra do Gargolo (r)

It's ironic that the smallest *autonomía* in Spain (in terms of population) should have the biggest reputation for its wines. A population of about 300,000 (half of whom live in the capital, Logroño) has its own single province, known until 1980 as Logroño, and self-governing as La Rioja since 1982. Previously it was seen as part of Castilla y León (Old Castile) but with strong influences from neighboring Basque-oriented Navarra and Álava. In the days before roads, the River Ebro, which flows through the north of the region and forms its boundary with the Basque Country and Navarra, was the main means of transportation between the Cantabrian Mountains and the Mediterranean.

La Rioja

Indeed, La Rioja has been one of the major crossroads of Spain since the *camino de Santiago*, the pilgrim route from France to the cathedral in Santiago de Compostela, was established in the ninth century. Pilgrims carrying the staff, scallop, and gourd of St. James still make the journey: 497 miles from the French border north of Roncesvalles, and 932 miles for the diehards who start their walk in Paris.

LOCAL SPECIALTIES

Although Rioja is famous for its lamb, beef (especially that certified by ASCRIVAC: the Beef and Cattle Breeders' Association of Rioja), and pork (and, inevitably, *jamón serrano*), it's also a rich source of fruit, vegetables, and confectionery. The town of Rincón de Soto in the east of the region is famous for its Blanquilla and Conference pears, which have their own DO, and the market-garden cauliflowers from Calahorra and its surrounding villages are protected, as are sweet peppers (*pimiento Riojano*) from the whole region, honey, cheese, wine vinegar, olive oil, and preserves and pickles made from horticultural products. Local protection extends to confectionery, cookies, *fardelejos* (a fried pastry-cake stuffed with marzipan), and the marzipan itself: *mazapán de Soto* from Soto en Cameros.

A typical traditional Riojan meal would, of course, begin with tapas, perhaps followed by *menestras* (a stew of seasonal vegetables, sometimes garnished with ham), then *embutidos*: spicy sausages, typically *chorizo* or *morcilla* (black pudding), often served with stuffed peppers; with a main course of *roast cordero* (lamb) or *cabrito* (kid). That's the simple food of La Rioja, although today there's a very much wider choice.

Using the very finest sausages in this straightforward recipe is the key to its deliciousness. Unlike most stews, which usually improve on reheating, *patatas a la Riojana* is best eaten immediately, so let it rest only briefly after cooking to give the sauce time to thicken.

Patatas a la Riojana

Potatoes cooked Riojan style

INGREDIENTS (SERVES 4)

1 tablespoon olive oil

3 garlic cloves, chopped

1 onion, finely chopped

1/2 chili pepper, finely chopped

1 green bell pepper, chopped

2lb 4oz potatoes, peeled and
   roughly chopped

7oz *chorizos*, sliced

salt and freshly ground black
   pepper, to taste

sprig of fresh thyme, to garnish

Heat the olive oil in a flameproof casserole, add the garlic and sauté until golden. Tip in the onion and sweat over a low heat until lightly browned. Then add the peppers. Sauté gently for 10 minutes, before adding the potatoes and *chorizos*. Stir all the ingredients together well and cover with cold water. Bring to a boil over a high heat, reduce to medium, and simmer for about 20 minutes until the potatoes are cooked. Season with salt and pepper.

Serve the potatoes and sauce in an earthenware dish, and pile the *chorizos*, peppers, and onion on top. Garnish with a sprig of fresh thyme.

WINE TIPS

SPECIAL OCCASION: **Finca Valpiedra, Rioja Alta (€€€)**
SUNDAY LUNCH: **Dominio de Ugarte, Heredad Ugarte, Rioja Alavesa (€€)**
EVERYDAY: **David Moreno Crianza. Rioja Alta (€)**

In Spain, the consumption of asparagus in La Rioja is three times higher than the national average. Not surprisingly, recipes making the most of this distinctively flavored vegetable abound. In this example, asparagus and green sweet peppers are teamed with hake, a lovely steaky white fish, and served with a traditional regional sauce.

Merluza frita sobre lecho de espárragos y pimientos con emulsión de guiso antiguo

Fried hake on a bed of asparagus and green peppers

INGREDIENTS (SERVES 4)

1lb 9oz hake fillets, cut into
   1¼ inch strips
all-purpose flour, lightly seasoned
   with salt and pepper
1 egg, beaten
3 tablespoons extra-virgin olive oil
3 green bell peppers
12 green asparagus spears
3 tablespoons olive oil
1 onion, chopped
1 garlic clove, chopped
1 carrot, chopped
1 cup short-grain rice
4 cups chicken stock
salt and pepper, to taste
3 scallions, finely sliced, to garnish

Roll the hake strips in the flour, then in the egg. Fry the strips for 60 seconds in a deep-fat fryer or a deep skillet containing plenty of sunflower oil over a high heat. Drain well on paper towels. Transfer to a skillet and fry over a medium heat for about 5 minutes. Remove from the skillet and set aside.

Heat the extra-virgin olive oil in a skillet, and fry the whole peppers, turning from time to time, until tender. Cover and set aside to cool, before peeling and cutting into strips.

Trim the asparagus spears and arrange the tips on a baking sheet. Brush with olive oil and place under a medium broiler for about 5 minutes until tender.

For the sauce, heat the olive oil in a saucepan, and sauté the onion and garlic until golden. Then add the carrot and rice and sauté for 2 minutes, before stirring in the chicken stock. Boil over a medium heat for 25 minutes. Season with salt and pepper, and mix well. Then push through a sieve to make the sauce.

Place some strips of green pepper on each plate and lay 3 asparagus tips on top. Arrange the pieces of hake on the bed of vegetables. Sprinkle with a little salt and garnish with some slices of scallion. Serve the sauce separately in a small pitcher.

WINE TIPS

SPECIAL OCCASION: **Viña Tondonia Gran Reserva Blanco, Rioja Alta (€€€)**
SUNDAY LUNCH: **Plácet, Palacios Remondo, Rioja Baja (€€)**
EVERYDAY: **Cosme Palacio Blanco Fermentado en Barrica, Palacio, Rioja Alavesa (€)**

Spanish kitchens specialize in serving top quality meat, which literally melts in the mouth, and meat doesn't come much sweeter or more tender than young lamb. This dish is a classic example of how the delicate flavor of the lamb can be enhanced with traditional fresh herbs. The indulgent twist of serving the lamb with truffled bread cubes introduces a modern edge to authentic Spanish fare.

Costillar de cordero lechal confitado en leche de oveja con romero, tomillo y migas trufadas

Marinated rack of young lamb with rosemary, thyme, and truffled bread cubes

INGREDIENTS (SERVES 4)

1 loaf of white bread, crusts removed, cut into small cubes

pinch of paprika

salt and pepper, to taste

3 tablespoons water

4oz streaky bacon slices, cut into small pieces

1 *chorizo* sausage, 8 inches long, chopped into small cubes

3 garlic cloves, chopped

1 rack of young lamb

4 cups sheep's milk

sprigs of fresh thyme

sprigs of fresh rosemary

1 tablespoon olive oil

truffle oil

1 black French truffle, very thinly sliced

sprigs of fresh thyme, to garnish

The night before, tip the bread cubes into a large bowl and sprinkle in the paprika, salt, pepper, and water. Toss well, then set aside overnight. Also, put the bacon and *chorizo* in a bowl, mix in the garlic, and leave overnight.

Early the next morning, remove the bones from the rack of lamb, making diagonal scores in the fat with a knife. Place the boneless piece of lamb in a roasting pan, and cover with the milk, rosemary, and thyme. Put in the oven and braise at 125°F for 10 hours. At the same time, put the bones in a roasting pan and roast in the oven for 4 hours until browned.

To make a sauce to serve with the lamb, transfer the bones to a large saucepan, cover with cold water, and bring to a boil. Simmer over a low heat for 30 minutes, then strain the stock into a clean saucepan. Continue simmering to reduce and thicken the stock. Season with salt and pepper.

When the lamb is cooked, cut into 4 portions and place each piece under a medium broiler for 5 minutes until the fat on top is browned.

Heat the olive oil in a large skillet or wok over a medium heat. Sauté the bacon, *chorizo*, and garlic until the bacon is browned. Then tip the bread cubes into the skillet. Turn off the heat and toss the bread with the bacon and *chorizo* to absorb all their flavors. Finally, drizzle over a little truffle oil and toss well.

Pile 2 tablespoons of the bacon, *chorizo*, and bread on each plate, with a few truffle shavings sprinkled over the top. Lean a piece of lamb on the pile, then pour a little sauce around the plate. Garnish with sprigs of fresh thyme.

WINE TIPS

SPECIAL OCCASION: **Hiru 3 Racimos, Luís Cañas, Rioja Alavesa (€€€)**
SUNDAY LUNCH: **Allende Tinto, Rioja Alta (€€)**
EVERYDAY: **Dinastía Vivanco Crianza, Rioja Alta (€)**

Swiss chard, artichokes, green beans, peas, asparagus, mushrooms, and borage are all cultivated in abundance in the gardens of La Rioja. Their flavors are so intense and fragrant that they can be used individually as an appetizer. In this very simple but well-balanced dish, for example, the borage gives the crunchy pork a real boost.

Borrajas salteadas con papada de cerdo
Sautéed borrajas *with pork cheeks*

INGREDIENTS (SERVES 4)

2lb 4oz *borrajas* (a green leafy vegetable with a white stem, similar to Swiss chard), washed and shredded

7oz pork cheeks

2 cups sunflower oil

salt and pepper, to taste

1 tablespoon olive oil

sprigs of fresh parsley, to garnish

Bring a large saucepan of salted water to a boil over a high heat. Drop in the *borrajas* and cook for about 15 minutes until tender. Let the leaves cool in the cooking water.

Meanwhile, preheat the oven to 225°F. Put the pork cheeks into a roasting tin, pour over the sunflower oil, and roast in the oven for 4 hours, or until cooked through.

Drain off the oil from the pork. Then brown the pork in a skillet, and cut into cubes.

Drain the *borrajas* well, season with salt and pepper, then drizzle over a little olive oil and toss to distribute evenly.

Place a deep metal ring in the center of each plate and pack in the borage. Then arrange the cubes of pork on top. Carefully remove the ring and garnish with sprigs of fresh parsley.

WINE TIPS

SPECIAL OCCASION: **Marques de la Concordia, Hacienda La Concordia, Rioja Baja (€€€)**
SUNDAY LUNCH: **Valenciso, Rioja Alta (€€)**
EVERYDAY: **Marqués de Cáceres Tinto, Rioja Alta (€)**

Wines of La Rioja

Rioja was the wine which changed Spanish winemaking in the 19th century. The two main pioneers were the Marqués de Murrieta in 1852 and the Marqués de Riscal in 1856, both of whom, quite separately, had lived in Bordeaux and studied the way wine was made there, and brought the technology back to La Rioja. It was a laborious and expensive endeavor, and their neighbors predicted financial disaster; however, fate intervened from the 1870s onward, when the phylloxera vine louse devastated the vineyards of France, and French *négociants* came to Rioja in search of wine to sell to their customers. They were delighted to find that "Bordeaux style" winemaking was turning out something recognizable in Rioja, and the first Rioja boom began. The French vineyards eventually recovered, of course, but the wines of Rioja remain a French favorite, particularly in the southwest.

Although the early pioneers brought Bordeaux vines to go with their Bordeaux technology (some Cabernet Sauvignon and Merlot vines are still found here and there) it was the triumph of the local Tempranillo grape that secured the future of Rioja wine, and it has since gone on to become Spain's flagship grape under various different names. Traditional Riojas use a mix of grapes: Tempranillo for fruit, Mazuelo for tannin and acidity, Graciano for structure, and Garnacha for strength and warmth. The right combination of these (every bodega has its own secret formula) makes wines of great finesse, style, elegance, and keeping-qualities. These days, however, as the market demands wines for more immediate drinking, there's a trend toward wines with 90 or even 100 percent Tempranillo which are drinkable a scant two years after the vintage and, in many cases, offer more of a snapshot of their *terroir* than the classic styles of wine.

In any case, the official back label of the bottle will tell you what to expect: *cosecha* (harvest) means that the wine has not been aged in oak, or alternatively that it's one of the new-wave "high-expression" wines (the price should indicate which

one); *crianza* means the wine has had at least a year in barrel and a year in bottle before release; *reserva* has had the same plus another year in barrel or bottle; *gran reserva* has had at least two years in barrel and at least three in bottle.

In today's market, Rioja can be divided into four main types. Of course, every bodega has its own house style, and many of them produce a range of wines across all styles, but, broadly speaking, this is what to expect:

Young wines with little or no oak have been made in Rioja since Roman times (the technology has moved on quite a bit since then), and in the Basque Country they are still the most favored style. Typically made with 100 percent Tempranillo, the wine is enjoyed young and fresh, sometimes as early as the Christmas after the vintage. In bars and cafés from Laguardia to Bilbao, the bright-purple liquid is drunk with great gusto from flat-bottomed tumblers, and elsewhere in Rioja most bars will have something similar in a house red.

Classic wines are the ones most people recognize as Rioja: full strawberry/raspberry Tempranillo fruit with a background of warm, toasty oak. These are the wines that built Rioja's reputation in the last quarter of the 19th century, and most mainstream houses make examples of them, labeled *crianza*, *reserva*, or *gran reserva* according to age. Perhaps the most classic of all Rioja bodegas is López de Heredia in Haro (www.lopezdeheredia.com), which is still making wine in much the same way as it did a century ago, and offering "current" vintages which are 10 and 15 years old.

Modern wines are those which tend to use the minimum oak to maximize the fruit and to allow for earlier drinking. The pioneer of this style was Marqués de Cáceres in Cenicero (www.marquesdecaceres.com), which installed the first all-stainless-steel bodega equipment in Rioja in the 1970s. Modern *crianza* wines often have the bare minimum 12 months in oak, and there are also wines which may be labeled *roble* that might have as few as three or four months in the barrel.

Genericos ("generic wines") started to appear in the late 1990s, and don't use the traditional descriptions (*crianza*, etc.). Typically these are very powerful, concentrated wines, and most winemakers claim that what they're trying to do is to get the maximum expression of the terroir into the wine. Two of the pioneers of this style are Roda and Allende (*see below*), and many mainstream bodegas now make a high-expression wine at the top of their range in addition to more traditional styles.

Indeed, given that it's now possible to find wines from the lightest, freshest, early-drinking gluggers to the most modern, blockbusting, high-expression wines, in addition to the ancient classics, there has never been a better time to enjoy Rioja.

OTHER WINES
VdlT Valles de Sadacia

Only in March, 2003, were the wines of the Valles de Sadacia classified as VdlT after years of lobbying by the five growers in the vineyards along the banks of the River Cidacos around Calahorra. Only two of these actually make wine, and the only example widely available is made under contract by a bodega in Logroño. They grow Moscatel with a little Malvasía and Viura, and the wines may be sweet, dry, or anything in between.

Main Bodegas

(listed in alphabetical order), PRODUCER NAME; town/village; web/E-mail address; best wines (r = red, w = white) A star (*) indicates particularly good quality.

DOCA RIOJA
www.riojawine.com
www.winesfromrioja.co.uk

Rioja is a generous wine in quality terms, and even the humblest bottle offers a level of reliability unparalleled in most other wine regions. In the selection below, however, constraints of space mean that only a very few of the best and most consistent bodegas can be included: the wines listed are those which have shown the highest quality in recent tastings.

AGRÍCOLA LABASTIDA; Labastida; www.agricolalabastida.com; El Belisario (r)*

ARTADI; Laguardia; www.artadi.com; Viña El Pisón (r)*; Pagos Viejos (r)*

BENJAMÍN ROMEO; San Vicente de la Sonsierra; contador@hotmail.com; Contador (*); La Viña de Andrés Romeo (r)*

BERONIA; Ollauri; www.beronia.es; III a.c. (r)*

BILBAÍNAS; Haro; www.bodegasbilbainas.com; La Vicalanda (r)*; Viña Pomal (r)*

BRETÓN; Navarette; www.bodegasbreton.com; Alba de Bretón (r)*; Dominio de Conte (r)*

CONTINO; Laserna-Laguardia; www.contino-sa.com; Graciano (r)*; Viña del Olivo (r)*

CVNE; Haro; www.cvne.com; Real de Asúa (*); Imperial (r)*

FINCA ALLENDE; Briones; www.finca-allende.com; Aurus (r)*; Calvario (r)*

FERNÁNDEZ DE MANZANOS; Azagra; www.bodegasfernandezdemanzanos.com; Finca Manzanos Crianza, Reserva (r)*

GUZMAN ALDAZÁBAL; Navaridas; guzmanaldazabal@terra.es; Exaltación (r)*; Guzmán Aldazábal (r)*

LÓPEZ DE HEREDIA; Haro; www.lopezdeheredia.com; Viña Tondonia Gran Reserva (rw)*

LUÍS CAÑAS; Villabuena; www.luiscanas.com; Hiru 3 Racimos (r)*; Amaren (r)*

MARQUÉS DE CÁCERES; Cenicero; www.marquesdecaceres.com; Gaudium (r)*; MC (r)*

MARQUÉS DE MURRIETA; Logroño; www.marquesdemurrieta.com; Dalmau (r)*; Reserva (r)*

MIGUEL MERINO; Briones; www.miguelmerino.com; Unnum (r)*; Magnum Gran Reserva (r)*

MUGA; Haro; www.bodegasmuga.es; Selección Especial (r)*; Prado Enea (r)*

OSTATU; Samaniego; www.ostatu.com; Gloria de Ostatu (r)*

PÁGANOS; Páganos-Laguardia; www.eguren.com; El Puntido (r)*; La Nieta (r)*

PALACIO; Laguardia; www.bodegaspalacio.es; Reserva Especial (r)*

PALACIOS REMONDO; Alfaro; www.palacioremondo.com; Plácet (w)*; Propriedad (r)*

PUJANZA; Laguardia; www.bodegaspujanza.com; Pujanza (r)*; Pujanza Norte (r)*

RAMÓN BILBAO; Haro; www.bodegasramonbilbao.es; Mirto (r)* REMELLURI; Labastida; www.remelluri.com; Colección Jaime Rodríguez (r)*; Reserva (r)*

REMÍREZ DE GANUZA; Samaniego; www.remirezdeganuza.com; Trasnocho (r)*; Reserva (r)*

RIOJANAS; Cenicero; www.bodegasriojanas.com; Gran Albina (r)*; Gran Albina Vendimia (r)*

RODA; Haro; www.roda.es; Cirsión (r)*; Roda I (r)*

SEÑORÍO DE SAN VICENTE; San Vicente de la Sonsierra; www.eguren.com; San Vicente (r)*

SIERRA CANTABRIA; San Vicente de la Sonsierra; www.eguren.com; Organza (w)*; El Bosque (r)*

TOBÍA; San Asensio; www.bodegastobia.com; Alma de Tobia (r)*; Óscar Tobía (r)*

VALDEMAR; Oyón; www.martinezbujanda.com; Inspiración Valdemar Graciano (r)*

VALSACRO; Pradejón; www.valsacro.com; Dioro (r)*; Valsacro (r)*

VdIT VALLES DE SADACIA

ONTAÑÓN; Logroño; www.ontanon.es; Marco Fabio (w)

Madrid is a thriving European capital of spacious boulevards and heroic fountains, large corporations, and long lunches. The teeming streets of the old town, dominated by the Plaza Mayor, are surrounded by architectural developments which date back to the early 19th century and give Madrid its cosmopolitan atmosphere. Yet Madrid is more than just a city: it's a province and an autonomous community with its own parliament.

From a food point of view, tapas are probably Madrid's staple diet; the bars around the Plaza Santa Ana are a particular magnet for lunchtime and early evening crowds before they hit the restaurants at about 9 p.m. where you can eat the food of every region of Spain, and most other

Madrid

countries, in the city. There are, however, some traditional dishes which survive here. One of the most famous is the *cocido madrileño*: a nourishing mix of vegetables and meat—indeed, anything poor families could find—which can be a hefty soup or a substantial stew.

LOCAL SPECIALTIES

Madrid has, however, not forgotten its gastronomic roots. Outside the city the countryside is rural, and known for its farms and smallholders.

A favorite is beef from the Sierra de Guadarrama north and west of the city, where they farm Avileña-Negra Ibérica, Limusina, and Charolais cattle.

Aceitunas de Campo Real are table olives (as opposed to olives for making oil) from Campo Real, which is about 22 miles east of the city. In terms of olive oil, *aceite de oliva virgen de Madrid* comes from olive groves in the southern part of the province.

Vegetables and fruit are legion, including *ajo blanco de Chinchón* ("white" garlic), *espárragos de Aranjuez* (asparagus), and *garbanzos y lentejas de Madrid* (beans and lentils). And there's a general classification, *hortalizas de Madrid*, for other vegetables seen as particularly good. *Melones de Villaconejos* (melons from Villaconejos), are grown 31 miles south of the city.

Dairy products include *queso de cabra* de Madrid (goat's cheese) and *queso puro de oveja de Madrid* (sheep's cheese), both from accredited farms. There's also a classified *leche pasteurizado de Madrid* for milk from accredited herds, as well as a category for *huevos de Madrid* (eggs).

Roasted suckling pig is one of the star dishes in the region of Madrid. In my family's restaurant, it's the only dish which, when properly cooked, reminds me that I belong to the third generation of chefs in the family. Each season, the flavor seems to change slightly, but the roasting technique remains the same. Cooking the pork in this way guarantees that the meat is not greasy and the crackling is very crunchy.

Cochinillo lacado sobre turrón de patata y almendra con tomillo limonero

Glazed suckling pig served on potato and almond nougat with lemon thyme

INGREDIENTS (SERVES 4)

1 piglet
6 tablespoons olive oil
salt, to taste
1 heaped tablespoon ground
    black pepper
6 tablespoons vinegar

FOR POTATO AND ALMOND NOUGAT

1lb 2oz potatoes, peeled and
    chopped
1 onion, chopped
extra-virgin olive oil
3/4 cup blanched almonds,
    roughly chopped
1 cup milk
1 teaspoon agar agar
salt and pepper, to taste
sprigs of fresh lemon thyme,
    to garnish

Make the potato and almond nougat the day before roasting the piglet. Preheat the oven to 140°F. Put the potatoes and onion in a roasting pan, cover with olive oil, and cook in the oven for 1 hour. Remove the potatoes and onions from the olive oil and drain in a colander.

Toast the almonds under the broiler until golden. Pour the milk into a flameproof casserole, add the almonds and potatoes, and bring to a boil over a high heat. Turn down the heat, and simmer until the potatoes start to break up. Stir in the agar agar, season with salt and pepper, and beat well. Pack the potato-almond mash into a shallow rectangular dish. Set aside to cool, before putting in the refrigerator for 24 hours.

The next day, preheat the oven to 400°F. Season the skin of the piglet with olive oil and salt, and inside the body cavity with salt, pepper, olive oil, and vinegar. Lay the piglet on its back in a heavy roasting pan and roast for 1 hour. Then turn the piglet over, taking care not to splash the hot fat, so its back faces upward. Roast for another hour until the skin is dark golden brown and the crackling crunchy. All the fat should drain to the bottom of the roasting pan.

When the piglet is cooked, remove from the oven and allow to rest for 10 minutes before serving. Turn the potato and almond nougat out of the dish onto a cutting board and cut into slices.

Place a slice of the potato and almond nougat on each plate, and put a piece of suckling pig on top. Garnish with a sprig of lemon thyme.

WINE TIPS

SPECIAL OCCASION: **El Rincón, Marqués de Griñón (€€€)**
SUNDAY LUNCH: **Montazo, Telmo Rodríguez (€€)**
EVERYDAY: **Maín Reserva, Orusco (€)**

Cooked properly, the *tortilla de patatas* (classic Spanish omelette) can be brilliant. In spite of its simple ingredients—eggs, potatoes, onions, and olive oil—it's an iconic dish, served in all the bars and restaurants in the region and city of Madrid. A good *tortilla* has to be moist, but never greasy. This exciting recipe pushes the boundaries of a homely dish to new horizons of taste, texture, and sophistication.

Tortilla en los pasos de la evolución
Evolutionary Spanish omelette

INGREDIENTS (SERVES 4)

FOR THE HOT POTATO FROTH
1lb 2oz potatoes, peeled and
  chopped
olive oil
1 cup heavy cream
pinch of salt
1 sifón iSi

FOR THE CARAMELIZED ONIONS
9oz onions, peeled, halved, and
  finely sliced
1/2 cup superfine sugar
olive oil

FOR THE SABAYON
3 egg yolks
pinch of salt
2 sheets of leaf gelatin, soaked in
  cold water
1 sifón iSi

GARNISH
sea salt crystals
fresh parsley, finely chopped

For the hot potato froth, preheat the oven to 165°F. Put the potatoes in a roasting pan, cover with olive oil, and cook in the oven for 2 hours.

To caramelize the onions, spread out the raw onions in a roasting pan and sprinkle with the sugar. Drench in olive oil, and cook gently in the same oven as the potatoes for at least 2 hours. Stir the onions frequently. (The success of the dish depends on turning the onions regularly.)

When the potatoes are cooked, drain off the olive oil and put the potato pieces in a food processor. Pour the cream into a saucepan and warm over a gentle heat, then pour over the potatoes in the food processor. Add the salt and blend thoroughly to form a smooth, runny puree. Pour into a cream-whipping siphon fitted with a nitrous oxide gas cylinder, and stand in a bain-marie to keep warm.

To make the sabayon (frothy egg whip), put the egg yolks in a bowl with a pinch of salt, and beat with a whisk. Add 1 tablespoon of hot water and whisk until the yolks have tripled in volume. Add the gelatin, and pour the mixture into another cream-whipping siphon fitted with a nitrous oxide gas cylinder. Stand the siphon in the top of a double-saucepan over simmering water to maintain a constant temperature.

Serve in heatproof cocktail glasses: a pina colada glass is the right shape to contain the two frothy elements. Put a teaspoon of the caramelized onions into each glass. Shake the sabayon siphon well, then squirt a burst of frothy sabayon over the onions. Then shake the potato siphon, and crown with a squirt of hot potato froth. Garnish with a pinch of sea salt and a sprinkling of parsley.

WINE TIPS

SPECIAL OCCASION: **750, Nueva Valverde (€€€)**
SUNDAY LUNCH: **Asido, Ricardo Benito (€€)**
EVERYDAY: **Puerta del Sol Varietales, Jeromín (€)**

This substantial dish appears in almost every old Madrid recipe book. Its origins can be traced back to the *olla podrida* (hotpot) from La Mancha. Traditionally, the stew is simmered for a long time over a low heat in an earthenware pot, although these days, when time is short, most people usually cook it in a pressure cooker.

Cocido Madrileño
Chickpea stew with vegetables and assorted meats

INGREDIENTS (SERVES 4)

2¹/3 cups dried chickpeas

1lb 5oz veal shank

1 piece of pig's knuckle

2 veal bones, with bone marrow

4oz salt pork

1 breast and 1 leg of chicken

1 onion, peeled and studded with
   2 cloves

6 carrots, peeled

4 potatoes, peeled

1/2 cabbage, coarsely shredded

10oz fine green beans

2 *chorizo* sausages, 8 inches long

2 *morcillas de cebolla*, or black
   pudding, 8 inches long

FOR THE DUMPLINGS

2 slices of bread, finely crumbed

1 egg

1 tablespoon chopped fresh
   parsley

1 garlic clove, crushed

meat stock

olive oil, for deep frying

1 garlic clove, crushed

pinch of salt

Put the chickpeas in a large bowl, cover with cold water, and soak overnight.

Rinse the veal, pig's knuckle, veal bones, and salt pork under cold running water. Trim any fat from the chicken. Place all the meat (except the chicken) in a large flameproof casserole, cover with water, and bring to a boil over a high heat. From time to time, skim off any residue that rises to the surface.

When the water is boiling, tip in the onion and chickpeas, and boil steadily for 1 hour. Then add the chicken, carrots, and potatoes, turn down the heat to low, and simmer gently for another hour, or until the meats are cooked through.

To make the dumplings, mix the bread crumbs, egg, parsley, and garlic together in a bowl, and add enough meat stock to make a stiff paste. Shape the paste into small balls, then fry in a skillet with plenty of olive oil, until golden all over. When the meat mixture has cooked for at least 2 hours, drop the dumplings into the casserole and simmer for another 30 minutes. Then drain off the stock into a separate saucepan, add a pinch of salt and serve as a soup.

Bring a saucepan of lightly salted cold water to a boil and drop in the cabbage and green beans. Boil for 15 minutes, then drain and set aside. Place the *chorizos* and *morcillas* in another saucepan with some hot meat stock from the casserole, and simmer for 30 minutes until heated through. Cut into smaller pieces and set aside.

This dish is usually served in three *vuelcos* (turns): as a soup, followed by servings of chickpeas, potatoes, cabbage, and green beans, and then the meat and sausages, with the dumplings alongside.

WINE TIPS

SPECIAL OCCASION: **Qubél Reserva, Gosálbez Orti (€€€)**

SUNDAY LUNCH: **Tagonius Crianza (€€)**

EVERYDAY: **Jesús Diaz Tinto (€)**

Migas, which literally translates as "bread crumbs," was originally a humble shepherds' dish, but from such tiny crumbs, some sensational desserts have been devised. In this particular sweet flight of fancy, *migas* is transformed into a trend-setting dessert, with a chocolate-flavored nutty crumble providing a crunchy contrast to creamy frozen yogurt and frothy white chocolate.

Migas de chocolate del siglo XXI

Twenty-first century chocolate "bread crumbs"

INGREDIENTS (SERVES 4)

FOR THE FROZEN YOGURT

6 tablespoons milk

3/4 cup heavy cream

1/2 cup superfine sugar

6 tablespoons Greek yogurt

4 tablespoons powdered yogurt

FOR THE *MIGAS*

1 cup butter, softened

2 cups all-purpose flour

3 tablespoons cocoa powder

1 cup light brown sugar

1 1/2 cups assorted blanched
   almonds and hazelnuts

FOR THE WHITE CHOCOLATE FROTH

1 cup milk

2/3 cup heavy cream

1 cup condensed milk

12oz white chocolate couverture
   (cooking chocolate)

3 sheets of leaf gelatin, soaked in
   cold water

1 sifón iSi

To make the frozen yogurt, put the milk, cream, and sugar in a saucepan and bring slowly to a boil over a medium heat, stirring constantly. Remove from the heat and allow to cool. Then stir in the fresh and powdered yogurts, pour into a plastic container and put in the freezer to set overnight.

To make the *migas*, preheat the oven to 375°F. Put the butter, flour, cocoa, sugar, and nuts in a food processor and blend for two 45-second bursts, or until the nuts are finely chopped. Then spread the crumble mixture onto a baking sheet with a spatula. Bake in the oven for 20 minutes. Remove from the oven and allow to cool slightly. While still warm, break up into fine crumbs with a fork.

For the white chocolate froth, pour the milk, cream, and condensed milk into a saucepan and bring to a boil. Take off the heat, add the white chocolate, and stir until melted. Then stir in the gelatin until it has dissolved. When cool, pour the chocolate cream into a cream-whipping siphon fitted with a nitrous oxide gas cylinder, and chill in the refrigerator. Shake the siphon well before piping the chocolate froth.

Pipe some white chocolate froth on one side of each bowl. In the center, pile up a heap of chocolate *migas*, and place a scoop of frozen yogurt beside the crumbs.

WINE TIPS

SPECIAL OCCASION: **Moscatel Chivite 125 (Navarra) (€€€)**

SUNDAY LUNCH: **Olivares Dulce Monastrell (Jumilla) (€€)**

EVERYDAY: **Blanco Semidulce Alma de Valdeguerra (€)**

Madrid wines and bodegas

Winemaking tradition in the Madrid area goes back to the 13th century, but the region wasn't promoted to full DO status until 1990 under the name *Vinos de Madrid* to avoid confusion with the *autonomía*, province, and city. This is the only DO zone in the province. On the face of it you'd expect a wine-producing area within the community of one of the world's largest capital cities to be fully geared up in terms of supplying its local market, but this has not been the case, partly because of the dominance of Rioja (as is the case all over Spain), partly, perhaps, because a prophet is always without honor in his own country, but mainly because, as recently as the mid-1990s, the wines were, quite simply, of no interest to anyone outside the village in which they had been made: perilously high in alcohol, boiled to death during fermentation, and often oxidized before they went into the bottle. Meanwhile, regions further afield, such as La Mancha and Valdepeñas, had leapfrogged the Madrid winelands to take the capital's café-bar market, while the city's best restaurants stuck to fine-wine areas such as Rioja and Ribera del Duero.

The regulations were changed in the late 1990s to allow for a more modern style, and work began on trying to persuade *Madrileños* to try the wines from their own community. After years of prejudice, that work is still going on, but there's no doubt that Madrid is now producing at least some world-class wines.

The vineyards of Madrid offer a range of qualities: here, there are wines which don't hit the high notes of the quality scale. There are also some excellent wines which are being vigorously marketed by the companies that make them, and are proud of them; a special mention must be made for Ricardo Benito, whose Divo is unquestionably one of the finest wines of Spain.

The DO's proximity to the city of Madrid, with its burgeoning market and ever-increasing prosperity, should provide all the stimulus necessary to get the best out of its growers and winemakers in the long term. The vineyards are high enough to avoid the worst of summer heat (Madrid city is the highest capital in Europe at 2,100 feet which provides an advantage in the ripening season (hot days and cold nights), and some stars are beginning to emerge among the DO's bodegas.

The vineyard area is split into three subzones in a kind of semicircle around the south of the city of Madrid, all named after the chief towns within them. Arganda is to the southeast, Navalcarnero to the west and south, and San Martín de Valdeiglesias to the west. The bodegas make all kinds of wine—red, pink, white, and sparkling—and also a local traditional wine in Arganda called *sobremadre* (literally "over mother"), which is fermented on its lees (the squashed grape skins and, indeed, "mother" of the wine) and left to mature in the tank for six months prior to bottling. It's hefty stuff.

For white, sweet, and sparkling wines, they grow the Malvar, Airén, Albillo, Viura, Parellada, Torrontés, and Moscatel grapes. For reds, there's Tempranillo (here known also as *Tinto Fino* and *Tinto de Madrid*), Garnacha, Merlot, Cabernet Sauvignon, Syrah, and Monastrell. The best wines are probably the reds made with Tempranillo, usually with a minority inclusion of Cabernet, Merlot, Syrah, and/or others. However, some interesting and good-value whites are made from the Malvar and barrel-fermented. This is an emerging region with great promise for the future, if star wines are a little few and far between at the moment.

OTHER DRINKS

The province of Madrid is also famous throughout Spain for an anise liqueur distilled in the town of Chinchón, about 25 miles southwest of the city. Both anise and grapes are grown locally; grape growers send their surplus wine for distillation, and green anise seeds are marinated in the spirit before it is redistilled in copper pot-stills. The spirit is made in several styles from dry (the strongest at over 70 percent abv; sometimes known colloquially as "brain-damage in a bottle") to sweet, with added sugar and at a lower strength. It's normally drunk as a *digestivo* after a meal, with water, ice, or even in coffee. It is rumored to have medicinal qualities and is popular with ladies "of a certain age" to alleviate arthritis. There is only one distillery remaining in Chinchón, and it now belongs to the Sherry giant González Byass (www.gonzalezbyass.com).

Main Bodegas

(listed in alphabetical order), PRODUCER NAME; town/village; web/E-mail address; best wines (r = red, w = white) A star (*) indicates particularly good quality.

Details of all bodegas are available at www.vinosdemadrid.es

RICARDO BENITO; Navalcarnero; www.ricardobenito.com; Divo (r)*, Tapon de Oro

NUEVA VALVERDE; Villa del Prado (San Martín de Valdeiglesias); www.bodegasnuevavalverde.com; Tejoneras (r), 750 (r)*

GOSÁLBEZ ORTI; Pozuelo del Rey (Arganda); www.qubel.com; Qubél (r)*

JEROMÍN; Villarejo de Salvanés (Arganda); www.vinosjeromin.com; Puerta del Sol (w), Félix Martin, Grego, Manu (r)*

TAGONIUS; Tielmes (Arganda); tagonius@reova.com; Tagonius (r)

Geographically, Murcia is part of the Levant, yet when the new regional Spain was created after the return to democracy, it became one of the seven single-province *autonomías*, independent of Valencia to the east and Castilla-La Mancha (New Castile) and Andalucía to the west. The reasons for this go back a long way. When the Moors were finally expelled from Spain in 1492, much of the land south of Madrid was scorched as a result of the battles between the Castilian and Moorish forces, and the crown offered land concessions to anyone prepared to move to this former war zone and cultivate it. Many people who had fled the war came back and restarted their farming lives, but they were Castilians and spoke Castellano. Over the border in Valencia they spoke (and still

Murcia

speak) Valençà, a dialect of Catalan, and this explains the difference: Levantine geography, Castilian culture and language.

This agricultural renascence has given the region a rich culture of farming which prevails to the present day. Murcia is the largest of the single-province *autonomías* and a great deal of its land is given over to food and wine production.

LOCAL SPECIALTIES

Meat products include the inevitable *jamón serrano* and *cordero* (lamb) *Segureña* (a local breed), plus cheese. *Queso de Murcia* is made from the milk of the local Murciano-Granadino goat, semihard and often flavored with rosemary and tarragon and it comes *fresco* (fresh), *curado* ("cured"—i.e. aged), and *al vino* (marinated in wine), and there's also a *queso de cabra curado á la almendra* (goat's cheese cured with almonds).

Murcia is a positive cornucopia of fresh produce: almost anything will grow in this fertile area. There is rice from Calasparra, about 44 miles northwest of Murcia city, pears from Jumilla (better known for its wine; see page 159), and region-wide production of *pimentón de Murcia*, red bell peppers of the Bola variety, dried and rendered into powder for cooking. Other produce grown across the region includes almonds, celery, broccoli, cauliflower, cabbage, chicory (frisée), lettuce, olives, and tomatoes. Fruits include citrus fruit, table grapes, melons, watermelons, and *frutales de hueso*: stone fruits such as plums, peaches, etc. In addition, of course, as with almost every other region of Spain, olive oil is a major product.

In the heartland of Murcia, vegetables reign supreme in dishes where freshness and eye-catching color are important. *Zarangollo* (an omelet) is a typical example of the Murcian approach to food. This avant-garde take on the *Zarangollo* is made without eggs and with the addition of fresh cod, which gives the dish an extremely stylish appearance and taste.

Zarangollo Murciano
Deconstructed tomato, potato, and vegetable mixture with cod and beets

INGREDIENTS (SERVES 4)
1 cup olive oil
2 onions, finely chopped
1 red bell pepper, finely chopped
3 tomatoes
1lb 2oz pumpkin, chopped
1lb 2oz potatoes, half roughly
    chopped, half cut into
    1¼ inch- thick slices
3 bay leaves
1 tablespoon agar agar
½ cup fresh dill
7oz cod fillet
4oz cooked beets
8 basil leaves
⅔ cup black tapioca pearls

FOR THE BISCAY SAUCE
4 garlic cloves, finely chopped
1 onion, finely chopped
7oz bread, cut into cubes
3 *choricero* peppers
1 cup all-purpose flour
1 cup chicken stock
salt and pepper, to taste

Heat 1 tablespoon of the olive oil in a skillet over a medium heat. Add the onions and pepper, sauté until softened but not browned, then set aside in a bowl. Skin, seed, and chop the tomatoes. Pour another 2 tablespoons of the olive oil into the skillet, and sauté the pumpkin, chopped potatoes, bay leaves, and tomatoes until cooked. Remove the bay leaves and put the vegetables and tomatoes into a food processor, add the agar agar and blend to a smooth puree.

Preheat the oven to 325°F. Put the sliced potatoes in an ovenproof dish with the dill and 3 tablespoons of the olive oil, and bake in the oven for 40 minutes until soft. Set aside. Put the cod in a separate ovenproof dish with 3 tablespoons of the olive oil and bake in the same oven for 15 minutes until just cooked. Allow to cool before flaking the cod, then set aside.

Thinly slice the cooked beets. Heat the remaining olive oil in a frying pan over a medium heat. Fry the slices of beet until crunchy. In the same oil, fry the basil leaves until crisp. Set both aside. Soften the tapioca in boiling water.

To make the Biscay sauce, heat 3 tablespoons of olive oil in a skillet over a medium heat. Add the garlic, onion, bread, and *choricero* peppers, and sauté until golden. Mix in the flour with a wooden spoon, then add the stock, and stir until the sauce thickens. Season with salt and pepper. Press through a sieve, leaving a sauce with a thick texture.

In the base of a dish, place 3 drops of the Biscay sauce, and on top of each, place some thick-sliced potato and then a portion of purée. On top of each portion, place a few slices of cod, and garnish with black tapioca pearls, beet, and basil.

WINE TIPS
SPECIAL OCCASION: **Clio, El Nido, Jumilla (€€€)**
SUNDAY LUNCH: **Partal Selección 37 Barricas, Balcona, Bullas (€€)**
EVERYDAY: **Castaño Monastrell, Yecla (€)**

With 106 miles of coastline, it **is hardly surprising that much of** Murcia's food **comes from** the sea. Fish such as horse mackerel, whitebait, and Atlantic mackerel often appear on the menu. Here, a popular delicacy, *pargo* (porgy or sea bream) is served with peaches, which **have been grown in the region since** Roman times.

Lomo de pargo asado con esencia de crustáceos y melocotón confitado

Broiled sea bream with shellfish essence and peach confit

INGREDIENTS (SERVES 4)

4lb 8oz sea bream, filleted

5 tomatoes, thickly sliced

2 onions, sliced

3 tablespoons pine nuts

4 garlic cloves, sliced

1 tablespoon chopped parsley

salt and pepper, to taste

2 cups olive oil

2 cups white wine

7oz green *piquillo* peppers

2 teaspoons dried oregano

2 teaspoons dried thyme

7oz each small crabs and spider crabs, cooked and shelled, shells saved

14oz shrimp, cooked and shelled, shells saved

14oz raw jumbo shrimp, shelled, shells saved

1/2 cup superfine sugar

2 peaches, sliced

1 teaspoon balsamic vinegar

1 teaspoon fresh thyme

1 teaspoon fresh rosemary

Preheat the oven to 350°F. Cut the fish fillets into 6oz pieces and place skin-side down in a roasting pan. Arrange the tomato and onion slices around the fish. Sprinkle the pine nuts on top with half the garlic. Sprinkle with chopped parsley, salt, and pepper. Drizzle with 2 tablespoons olive oil, and pour the wine on top along with 1¼ pint water. Put the roasting pan in an oven for about 15 minutes until the fish is cooked.

Meanwhile, put the *piquillo* peppers on a baking sheet and roast in the oven for 12 minutes. Then tip into a food processor and blend to a puree. Strain the puree to remove skin, seeds, and stalk. Remove the soft flesh from the remaining tomatoes, puree them, add to the pepper puree, and season with the oregano and thyme.

Put the shells of the crabs and shrimp into a saucepan and barely cover with water. Bring to a boil, then simmer on a low heat for 20 minutes to make a stock. Strain through a sieve into a clean saucepan, and reduce over a low heat to make a sauce.

In a small saucepan, stir the superfine sugar and 3 tablespoons cold water together over a high heat until the sugar has dissolved (about 6 minutes). Add the peaches and cook for an additional 2 minutes until you have a golden, caramelized syrup. Set aside.

Heat 2 tablespoons of olive oil in a skillet, and fry the garlic until crunchy. Arrange the jumbo shrimp on a tray, brush with olive oil, and put under a medium broiler for 4 minutes, turning once, until pink all over.

Draw a few lines with the pepper puree in the middle of a plate. Place a piece of fish in the center, arrange 5 peach slices around it, and place the shrimp and crab on top. Bathe in reduced fish stock. Garnish with a drizzle of balsamic vinegar and olive oil, the crunchy garlic, and fresh rosemary and thyme.

WINE TIPS

SPECIAL OCCASION: **Manuel Manzaneque Chardonnay, Finca Élez (DO Pago) (€€€)**

SUNDAY LUNCH: **Casa de la Ermita Viognier, Jumilla (€€)**

EVERYDAY: **Valcorso fermentado en barrica, La Purísima, Yecla (€)**

Better known as a tourist destination for watersports enthusiasts, the maritime lagoon of the Mar Menor is also one of the finest fishing areas for catching jumbo shrimp and gray mussels. Regional seafood plays a leading role in this recipe, together with the rice of Calasparra, whose short, plump grains are capable of absorbing intense flavors.

Arroz meloso de Calasparra con langostino del Mar Menor y queso al aroma de vino tinto

Sweet Calasparra rice with jumbo shrimp and wine-scented cheese

INGREDIENTS (SERVES 4)

10oz fish bones

2 cups water

2 garlic cloves

2 cups fresh parsley, chopped

1 1/2 cups olive oil

2 onions, chopped

1 tablespoon all-purpose flour

1 cup white wine

1/2 cup squid ink

salt and pepper, to taste

a few sprigs of fresh parsley

1 cup red wine

1 1/2 cups Calasparra rice

2 cups hot beef stock

1/4 cup cream cheese

1 tablespoon raisins, marinated in sweet red wine

1 tablespoon pine nuts

14oz raw jumbo shrimp, peeled

To make a fish stock, put the fish bones and water in a large saucepan. Bring to a boil over a high heat, then simmer over a low heat for 30 minutes. Strain the stock through a sieve into a clean saucepan over a very low heat to keep warm. Grind the garlic and parsley to a paste in a mortar and pestle.

Heat 2 tablespoons olive oil in a large saucepan over a medium heat and sauté the onion. Mix the flour into the skillet with a wooden spoon, and cook for 1 minute. Add the white wine, stirring continuously as the sauce thickens. Gradually stir in half the ground garlic and parsley, and enough fish stock to thin the sauce. When the sauce begins to boil, add the squid ink, salt, and pepper. Turn down the heat to low, simmer gently until the sauce thickens, and set aside.

Blend the parsley sprigs with 1 cup of olive oil in a food processor for 1 minute to make an oil. Bring the red wine to a boil in a skillet, reduce the heat, and simmer until thickened.

Heat 4 tablespoons of olive oil in a saucepan, and sauté the remaining ground garlic and parsley. Stir in the rice, then gradually add the beef stock: add 1/2 cup at a time, stirring continuously, and wait until the stock has been absorbed by the rice before adding more. When all the beef stock has been added, use some of the remaining hot fish stock to keep the rice moist until cooked. Then stir in the cream cheese, raisins, pine nuts, and season with salt and pepper. Brush the the jumbo shrimp with the remaining olive oil and broil for 4 minutes, turning, until pink all over.

Spoon a trail of squid ink base across each plate. Spoon some of the rice on top, and crown with the jumbo shrimp. Drizzle some parsley oil and red wine reduction around the plates before serving.

WINE TIPS

SPECIAL OCCASION: **Viña Tondonia Rosado Crianza (Rioja) (€€€)**
SUNDAY LUNCH: **Alceño Rosado, Pedro Luís Martínez, Jumilla (€€)**
EVERYDAY: **Castillo de Jumilla Monastrell Rosado, Bleda, Jumilla (€)**

Paparajotes are always served on St. George's Day, which is celebrated on March 19 in Spain. This unusual Murcian dessert is made with lemon leaves. Although the leaves are never eaten, they form a platform on which to fry the batter and infuse it with a sublime lemon flavor. This dessert is typical of the *barracas* (urban open-air cafés), which suddenly pop up in Murcia with the arrival of spring.

Paparajotes
Lemon leaves deep-fried with eggs and cinnamon

INGREDIENTS (SERVES 4)

4 cups milk

3 cups water

6 eggs, separated

4¹/2 cups self-rising flour

juice of 1 lemon

ground cinnamon, to taste

3 cups superfine sugar

2 cups vegetable oil

24 lemon leaves, washed

2 tablespoons confectioners' sugar
    and 1 teaspoon cinnamon, sifted
    together, for dusting the leaves
    and for the sweet spicy milk

7oz Emmental cheese, diced

2 tablespoons all-purpose flour

1 egg, well beaten

¹/3 cup blueberry jelly

2 tablespoons agar agar

4 sheets of leaf gelatin, soaked

1 iSi siphon

13/4 cups fresh red currants

¹/2 cup fresh mint

Beat together 3¹/3 cups milk, the water, and egg yolks in a bowl. Sprinkle in the flour gradually, beating to stop lumps forming. Beat in the lemon juice, cinnamon, and 2 cups sugar. Beat the egg whites into stiff peaks, and fold into the batter. Heat the oil in a saucepan. Dip the lemon leaves in the batter and fry in batches until crisp and golden. Drain on paper towels. Dust with confectioners' sugar and cinnamon.

Toss the Emmental cheese in flour, then dip in egg, and fry for a few seconds in very hot oil. Drain on paper towels and set aside.

To make a syrup, put the remaining sugar and 3 tablespoons of water in a saucepan. Heat, over a medium heat, stirring until the sugar dissolves, then allow to simmer until fine strands form. Stir in the jelly and agar agar until dissolved. Pour the mixture into a small rectangular dish, and chill until set—it should be translucent and soft but firm.

Put the remaining milk, cinnamon, and confectioners' sugar, into a *thermomix* (food processor that also cooks). Blend at speed 6 at 210°F for 5 minutes. Add the gelatin and blend for 3 more minutes. Pour the sweet spicy milk into a cream-whipping siphon fitted with a nitrous oxide gas cylinder, and set aside to cool for 2 hours.

Make a caramel to glaze the red currants. In a small saucepan, stir ¹/2 cup superfine sugar and 6 tablespoons cold water together over a high heat until the sugar has dissolved. Continue to heat until the syrup is golden. Remove from the heat immediately and carefully dip the bunches of red currants into the caramel.

Put a slice of the blueberry jelly and a few Emmental cubes on each plate. Arrange 6 crisp battered lemon leaves on top. Finish with a cloud of cinnamon froth and the caramelized red currants. Garnish with a few sprigs of fresh mint.

WINE TIPS

SPECIAL OCCASION: **Castaño Monastrell Dulce, Yecla (€€€)**

SUNDAY LUNCH: **Dulce María Jesús de Castilla Luzón, Jumilla (€€)**

EVERYDAY: **Casa de la Ermita Dulce, Jumilla (€)**

Wines of Murcia

Murcia is something of a newcomer to wine production at an international level. Although the Jumilla DO was created in 1966, it didn't produce anything of note until the mid-1990s. The same applies to Yecla (1975), whose rise to fame is thanks largely to the efforts of one bodega (Castaño) which drove quality forward at a time when few importers were interested in emergent regions. The most recent addition is Bullas (1994) and it has jumped on the quality bandwagon created by its two neighbors.

The main grape is the Monastrell (aka Mourvèdre), which was always used to make high-strength wines to be sold to other regions (and other countries) to beef up thin reds. In the early 1990s, somebody dared to try something original with the grape, and it proved to have hidden depths: richness, power, even a bit of elegance when treated with respect. Since then, Tempranillo and Garnacha have increased in area, and Cabernet Sauvignon, Merlot, and Syrah have been introduced, with sometimes blockbusting effect. There are also white wines made from Airén, Macabeo, and Pedro Ximénez, but in this hot, southern climate the reds tend to dominate.

DO BULLAS
A large area, occupying most of the western half of Murcia. The vineyards can be high: from 1,312 to 2,625 feet. Main grapes are the Monastrell and Tempranillo, and wines are mainly red.

DO JUMILLA
Around the town of the same name, this was the flame that lit the beacon for Murcia in about 1994, with the news that the Monastrell grape really could compete.

DO YECLA
The only DO in Spain relating to a single town, this is another whose best wines also tend to be made from Monastrell.

OTHER WINES
There are two country-wine areas in Murcia. VdlT Campo de Cartagena on the southeast coast makes sweet wines from Tempranillo and Monastrell. VdlT Abanilla, adjacent to the Alicante DO, makes red and white wines of everyday quality.

Main Bodegas
(listed in alphabetical order), PRODUCER NAME; town/village; web/E-mail address; best wines (r = red, w = white)
A star (*) indicates particularly good quality.

DO BULLAS
www.bullas.es/vino

BALCONA; Cehegín; www.partal-vinos.com; Partal (r)

DO JUMILLA
www.crdo-jumilla.com

AGAPITO RICO; Jumilla; www.carchelo.com; Carchelo (r)*

BLEDA; Jumilla; www.bodegasbleda.com; Castillo de Jumilla (r)

CASA DE LA ERMITA; Jumilla; www.casadelaermita.com; Monasterio de Santa Ana (r)* Casa de la Ermita Reserva (r)*

EL NIDO; Jumilla; www.bodegaselnido.com; El Nido (r)*, Clio (r)*

JULIA ROCH E HIJOS; Jumilla; www.casacastillo.es; Casa Castillo Pie Franco (r)*

LUZÓN; Jumilla; www.bodegasluzon.com; Altos de Luzón (r)*, Castillo de Luzón (r)

DO YECLA
www.yeclavino.com

CASTAÑO; Yecla; www.bodegascastano.com; Viña al Lado de la Casa (r)*, Monastrell Dulce (sweet r)*

LA PURÍSIMA; Yecla; www.calpyecla.com; Trapio (r), Iglesia Vieja (r)

A thousand years ago, the Kingdom of Navarre covered most of northern Spain between Galicia and Barcelona as well as a sizable slice of southwestern France. Over the next several centuries it changed hands a number of times. Indeed, Louis XVI of France styled himself "King of France and Navarre" until 1792. In the meantime, the original kingdom had shrunk to become the region we know today as Navarra, and, in return for a royal charter, it agreed to become part of Spain in 1512. Today, it's a single-province, self-governing region, and one of the most prosperous in Spain. Part of its early prosperity was thanks to the Camino de Santiago, the first "tourist route" in Europe, which brought pilgrims and churchmen from all over the Continent heading for Santiago de Compostela. Shakespeare set his play *Love's Labours Lost* in what was then Navarre, and the opening speech declares "Navarre shall be the wonder of the world!" .

Navarra

LOCAL SPECIALTIES

Navarra has always been one of the *huertas* (market gardens) of Spain: a richly fertile landscape where anything from asparagus to olive trees will thrive. *Esparragós de Navarra* (a *denominación* shared with neighboring Aragón), the famous white asparagus which is grown underground, is eaten fresh from March to June but usually bottled or tinned for consumption all the year round. *Alcachofa de Tudela* is a special variety of globe artichoke grown in 32 towns and villages

around Tudela, in the deep south of the region, harvested sometimes as early as February. *Pimiento del piquillo de Lodosa* comes from eight villages around Lodosa, near the border with La Rioja. The peppers are a species unique to Navarra, and are eaten fresh and roasted as well as being bottled and tinned.

Navarra is livestock-farming country, too, and *ternera de Navarra* is beef taken from the native Pirenaica cattle, believed to have originated in northern Navarra. *Cordero de Navarra* is lamb from anywhere in the region, from the Navarra and Lacha/Latxa (mainly in the north) breeds. These same sheep provide milk for the cheese from Roncal; they graze the high pastures of the Pyrenees, and the cheese is made from December to July: firm without being hard, with a strong, spicy flavor.

Navarra is also renowned for its dairy products: Idiazábal is probably the region's most famous cheese. It's made from the unpasteurized milk of Latxa and Carranzana sheep, grazed in the Pyrenees. When mature, the cheese is crumbly, with a sharp, pungent aroma. In this ingenious recipe, the intense piquant flavor of the Idiazábal cheese acts as the perfect foil for the salty ham and tender baby broad beans.

Cuaja de queso Idiazábal sobre habitas salteadas con jamón Ibérico

Idiazábal curd cheese with baby fava beans and Iberian ham

INGREDIENTS (SERVES 4)

1 handful of fresh mint, chopped

2 tablespoons olive oil

2/2 cup fresh baby fava beans, pods removed

4oz Iberian or *serrano* ham, chopped

FOR THE CURD CHEESE

1¼ cups milk

14oz Idiazábal cheese, grated

1¼ cups heavy cream

7 sheets of leaf gelatin, soaked in cold water

1 cream-whipping siphon, fitted with 2 nitrous oxide gas cylinders

toasted spiced bread, to serve (optional)

For the curd cheese, pour the milk into a saucepan and bring to boiling point over a medium heat. Then remove from the heat and add the cheese to the hot milk, without stirring. Set aside to infuse and cool for 30 minutes.

When cold, stir in the cream and strain through a sieve into a clean saucepan. Return to the heat and warm gently over a low heat. Add the gelatin and stir until dissolved. Pour into a cream-whipping siphon fitted with 2 nitrous oxide gas cylinders, and set aside to cool. Put in the refrigerator to set.

Put the mint in a bowl, cover with olive oil, and allow to infuse for 15 minutes.

Blanch the fava beans in a saucepan of boiling water for 5 minutes. Drain off the hot water and cool quickly under cold running water. Then peel the skin off every bean. Transfer to a bowl and toss with a drizzle of mint oil.

Heat 2 tablespoons of olive oil in a skillet over a medium heat and sauté the ham until it is crisp. Squirt some curd cheese out of the siphon into each of the cocktail glasses, to half fill them. Put 2 teaspoons of the warm sautéed bean and ham mixture on top of the chilled curd, and crown with a thin slice of toasted spiced bread, if desired.

WINE TIPS

SPECIAL OCCASION: **Lautus, Guelbenzu, Ribera del Queiles (€€€)**

SUNDAY LUNCH: **Castillo de Monjardín Reserva, Navarra (€€)**

EVERYDAY: **Ochoa Cabernet-Sauvignon, Navarra (€)**

Fresh vegetables feature prominently in Navarran cuisine. Much is made of the *piquillo* pepper: a small variety, with a red skin and meaty texture. The *piquillos* are harvested in the fall, roasted over wood fires, then peeled by hand and preserved whole in jars of olive oil, which gives them a unique flavor and texture that can be enjoyed throughout the year.

Alcachofas de Tudela con asado de pimiento de piquillo de Lodosa y borrajas al carbón

Tudela artichokes with chargrilled peppers and borage

INGREDIENTS (SERVES 4)

8 fresh baby globe artichokes

juice of 1 lemon

salt, to taste

5 cups fresh parsley

7oz *borrajas* (a green leafy
   vegetable similar to
   Swiss chard), shredded

7oz jar of *Pimientos del piquillo*
   (*piquillo* peppers)

1 tablespoon olive oil

1 cup slivered almonds, cut
   into shreds

pinch of *polvo de humo* (hickory
   smoked powder)

To prepare the artichokes, cut through the equator with a sharp knife and throw away the tops. Pull out the tough leaves around the base and discard. Carefully peel the stem and trim off all the remaining tough outer green leaves around the sides and base until left with only the white part. Dig out the inedible hairy choke in the middle with a spoon and discard. (Artichoke hearts go black very quickly when peeled and exposed to air. To prevent discoloration, pour half the lemon juice into a bowl of cold water and keep dunking the artichoke in the acidulated water.)

To cook the artichokes, put the hearts, with stalks attached, into a stainless-steel saucepan, cover with water, and add the lemon juice, salt, and parsley. Bring to a boil over a high heat, then remove from the heat and allow to cool in the water.

Blanch the *borrajas* in a saucepan of lightly salted boiling water, then cool quickly under a running tap. Drain well in a colander and set aside.

Drain the olive oil from the *piquillos*. Remove the seeds and stems, place in a food processor and blend to a smooth puree.

Heat the olive oil in a skillet over a medium heat. Sauté the almonds until lightly browned, and mix in the borage and *polvo de humo*.

Arrange 2 artichoke hearts on each plate, with the stalks pointing upward. Pile the smoky almonds and *borrajas* on top, and spoon a little pepper puree to one side.

WINE TIPS

SPECIAL OCCASION: **Conde de la Vega Reserva, Palacio de la Vega, Navarra (€€€)**
SUNDAY LUNCH: **Principe de Viana 1423, Navarra (€€)**
EVERYDAY: **Señorío de Sarría Reserva, Navarra (€)**

Another boldly-flavored cheese made from unpasteurized sheep's milk is produced in the Roncal Valley region of Navarra. It's a hard, ivory-colored cheese with holes, which has a creamy texture and a strong, slightly spicy taste. This recipe was designed to highlight its unique flavor. Eating fresh asparagus with Roncal cheese is a truly inspired and mouthwatering combination.

Espárragos blancos en tempura con mayonesa de queso de Roncal

White asparagus tempura with Roncal cheese mayonnaise

INGREDIENTS (SERVES 4)
20 spears white asparagus
7oz Roncal cheese, Manchego, or any other hard sheep's cheese, finely grated

FOR THE TEMPURA BATTER
2 1/2 tablespoons easy-blend dry yeast
1 cup all-purpose flour
1 teaspoon salt
1 teaspoon superfine sugar
2 cups warm water

FOR THE MAYONNAISE
3 eggs
2 egg yolks
1 teaspoon Dijon mustard
1 1/4 cups sunflower oil
5 tablespoons olive oil
1 teaspoon Sherry wine vinegar
1 cream-whipping siphon fitted with 2 nitrous oxide gas cylinders
olive oil, for frying

Make the tempura batter by combining all the ingredients, except the water, in a large bowl and mix well. Stir in the water and leave in a warm place to ferment until required.

For the mayonnaise, beat all the ingredients together until the mixture has a thick texture. Put in the cream-whipping siphon fitted with 2 nitrous oxide gas cylinders and set aside in a cool place.

Cut the asparagus spears in half lengthwise. Bring a large saucepan of water to a boil, drop in the asparagus and blanch briefly for 2 minutes. Remove from the water, cool under cold running water, and dry well on a clean dish towel.

Heat plenty of olive oil in a large saucepan or wok, and cook over a high heat until a drop of batter starts frying as soon as it hits the hot oil. Dip each asparagus spear in the tempura batter and fry for about 60 seconds until golden and crisp. Carefully remove from the olive oil, and drain on paper towels.

Pipe the mayonnaise from the siphon into a bowl and fold in the cheese.

Arrange 10 asparagus spears on each plate. Serve with a bowl of the cheesy mayonnaise froth.

WINE TIPS
SPECIAL OCCASION: **Colección 125 Tinto Reserva, Chivite, Navarra (€€€)**
SUNDAY LUNCH: **Barón de Magaña, Navarra (€€)**
EVERYDAY: **Azul, Guelbenzu, Ribera del Queiles (€)**

The neighboring Basque Country helps to account for the abundance and freshness of the seafood that plays such a prominent role in Navarran cuisine. One of the most popular items is baby squid, which is eaten everywhere in the taverns and restaurants, accompanied by local wines. In this recipe, the fresh black pasta and the aroma of truffles produces a dish that tastes as good as it looks.

Lasaña de chipirones con aceite de trufa y majado de cebollino y aguacate

Baby squid lasagna with truffle oil, and avocado and scallion salsa

INGREDIENTS (SERVES 4)

8 sheets of fresh lasagna made with squid ink
3 tablespoons olive oil
1 teaspoon salt
32 baby squid
2 avocados, finely chopped
5 scallions, finely sliced
4 teaspoons squid ink
3 tablespoons sunflower oil
1 tablespoon olive oil
1 onion, thinly sliced
2 tablespoons truffle oil

Put plenty of water in a saucepan, add 1 tablespoon of olive oil and the salt, and bring to a boil over a high heat. Cook the pasta for about 5 minutes.

Put the cleaned squid under a medium broiler for 15 minutes until browned, turning halfway through the cooking time.

Meanwhile, mix the avocados, scallions, and 1 tablespoon olive oil together to make a salsa.

Pour the squid ink into a bowl and beat in the sunflower oil to make a vinaigrette.

Heat the remaining olive oil in a skillet and fry the onion until very crunchy.

Lay a sheet of lasagna on each plate, top with 8 baby squid, a little of the crunchy onion, and some avocado and scallion salsa. Pour a drizzle of truffle oil on top, and cover with another sheet of pasta. Finish off with a little more avocado and scallion salsa, some strands of crunchy onion and the remaining squid. Drizzle the squid ink vinaigrette around the plate.

WINE TIPS

SPECIAL OCCASION: **Colección 125 Banco Reserva, Chivite, Navarra (€€€)**
SUNDAY LUNCH: **Palacio de Otazu Fermentado en Barrica, Navarra (€€)**
EVERYDAY: **Monte Cristo, Camilo Castilla, Navarra (€)**

Wines of Navarra

The DO Navarra was established in 1958, but it's only since the late 1980s that the region has really started to makes its name known in the outside world. Historically, Navarra grew Garnacha grapes and made rosado (rosé) wine, even though its best wines have always been red. In the 1970s and 1980s, importers in other countries (notably the U.K.) started to market the red wines of Navarra as being "very similar to Rioja but quite a bit cheaper," but this didn't help profitability or investment, either.

The largest and oldest (1647) bodega in the region is Julián Chivite; even in the mid-1980s it accounted for more than 50 percent of all wine exported from Navarra. The 1990s, however, saw a big increase in inward investment, partly due to the support provided by the conseja regulador, or regulatory body, which had liberalized the regulations and made it possible to grow a wide range of grapes and experiment with more modern styles of winemaking. As a result, although Garnacha and Tempranillo are still prominent, the vineyard now has Cabernet Sauvignon and Merlot, with Chardonnay and Moscatel for whites. The last has achieved cult status in recent years, and a number of bodegas (notably Camilo Castilla, Ochoa, and Chivite) are turning out world-class examples of sweet wines made from it, some of them lightly fortified.

Navarra's main strength, however, is its reds and, to a lesser extent whites. Garnacha is still the most widely planted grape, but you're as likely to find wines made from 100 percent Cabernet Sauvignon, Cabernet-Merlot mixes, and even the odd Pinot Noir—there are some three dozen experimental varieties being trialed at any one time. Red wines which seem to do best in international tastings tend to be about two-thirds Tempranillo and a third Cabernet and/or Merlot. For whites, Chardonnay has made its home here with a vengeance, and some of Navarra's finest whites are, typically, barrel-fermented with anything up to a year in the barrel afterwards. A cheaper option is to blend in some Viura: the more there is, the lower the price. And, of course, good old rosado hasn't gone away.

Garnacha turns out delicious, easy-drinking wines made by the sangrado method, in which the grapes are crushed and left on the skins for anything from a few hours to a day and the juice is run off when the winemaker decides the color is right.

NB: the southeastern part of Navarra produces wines under the DOCa Rioja, and these are discussed in the chapter on La Rioja.

OTHER WINES
VdlT Ribera del Queiles

A cross-border VdlT area, following the tiny River Queiles, which flows into Navarra from Aragón (*see* Aragón, page 30). It was created as a result of the Guelbenzu family's desire to make a wine under their own name from grapes grown on both sides of the border. This is forbidden under DO regulations, so they withdrew from the Navarra DO in 2003 and started calling their wine by this name. It was confirmed officially in 2005, even though they are still the only producer.

OTHER DRINKS

Pacharán, or *Patxaran*, is an anise-flavored spirit made all over northern Spain, but it originated in Navarra and has ties with other flavored spirits made in southern France, going back to the days of the Kingdom of Navarre. Anise is not the only ingredient; the main fruit controlled by the consejo regulador is sloes, which are macerated in pure alcohol for anything from one to eight months. The anise is added before and after the process, and many producers have secret ingredients which they add to give the final flavor. Pacharán may be anything from clear to pink to almost red in color, depending on the length of maceration of the sloes, and it may be sweet, dry, or anything in between. Typically 25 to 30 percent alcohol, it's drunk as an *aperitivo* or a *digestivo*, depending on the sweetness or personal preference.

Main Bodegas

(listed in alphabetical order), PRODUCER NAME; town/village; web/E-mail address; best wines (r = red, w = white)
A star (*) indicates particularly good quality.

ARTADI; Artazu; www.artadi.com; Artazuri (r), Santa Cruz de Artazu (r)*

CAMILO CASTILLA; Corella; www.bodegascamilocastilla.com; Capricho de Goya (sweet w)*, Moscatel Montecristo (sweet w)*

CASTILLO DE MONJARDÍN; Villamayor de Monjardín; www.monjardin.es; Castillo de Monjardín (rw)

IRACHE; Ayegui; www.irache.com; Castillo Irache (r)

JULIÁN CHIVITE; Cintruenigo; www.bodegaschivite.com; Colección 125 (rw)*, Gran Feudo Viñas Viejas (r)*

LUÍS GURPEGUI MUGA; San Adrián; Monty Ory (r)

NEKEAS; Añorbe; www.nekeas.com; Izar de Nekeas (r)

OCHOA; Olite; www.bodegasochoa.com; Ochoa (rw), Dulce (sweet w)*

OTAZU; Echaurri; www.otazu.com; Palacio de Otazu (r)

PRÍNCIPE DE VIANA; Murchante; www.principedeviana.com; Principe de Viana (rpw)

SARRÍA; Puente la Reina; www.bodegadesarria.com; Señorio de Sarria (rw)

VINÍCOLA DE NAVARRA; Tiebas; www.domecqbodegas.com; Castillo de Javier (r), Las Campanas Reserva (r)

País Vasco, or The Basque Country in English, (Euskadi in Basque) is an area famous for heavy industry, shipbuilding, and exports, and it remains one of the most prosperous regions in the whole of Europe. Historically, the area covered land in France (Gascony) and Spain, and under the Franco régime, Basque language and culture were suppressed. Since the constitution of 1978, however, it has been an autonomous community within Spain. There are three provinces: Vizcaya (Bizkaia) on the north coast, whose capital is Bilbao (Bilbo); Guipúzcoa (Gipuzkoa) to the east along the coast to the French border, whose capital is San Sebastián (Donostia); and to the south behind the Cantabrian Mountains, Álava (Araba), whose capital is Vitoria (Gasteiz).

LOCAL SPECIALTIES

Food is central to Basque life, and Basque cookery is reckoned among the best in the world. There's an understandable emphasis on high-quality ingredients: fish, meat, cheese, fruit, and vegetables are produced

País Vasco

here in abundance and at very high-quality levels. In addition to the national system of *denominaciones*, the Basque government awards its own "Eusko" label to quality products.

Idiazábal is the region's most famous cheese, made from the milk of Lacha and Carranzana sheep. Traditionally smoked over beech wood, it also comes unsmoked, and ages well, becoming crumbly when mature. *Pollo de Caserío Vasco* (Basque farmhouse chicken) is a protected breed of fowl which lives a free-range life, is fed mainly on corn, and is claimed to represent the real taste of old country-style chicken. *Cordero lechal del País Vasco* is milk-fed baby lamb of the same breeds which produce *idiazábal* cheese, only available seasonally; *carne de vacuno del País Vasco* is beef from cattle from certified herds, available only through selected butchers.

Fruit and vegetables abound, with protected status for the organic *patata* (potato) *de Álava*, the long green sweet peppers of Gernika (*pimineto de Gernika*), *guindillas* (chili peppers) *de Ibarra*, and *tomate de calidad del País Vasco*—farm-grown tomatoes with a unique, traditional taste. There are three categories for navy beans alone: *alubia pinta Alavesa*, *alubia de Gernika*, and *alubia de Tolosa*. The *Euskal Baserri* label guarantees farm produce, grown locally to strict standards.

With such a long coastline, fishing has always been a primary industry, and the local tuna (*bonito del norte y cimarrón*), traditionally fished with rod and line, is also protected, as is the local honey. The Basques take their food very seriously.

Fortunately, looks aren't everything where the large-scaled scorpionfish is concerned: it may be one of the ugliest fish in the world, but it tastes delicious. In Spain, it's known by various names: in Castile and Asturias, they call it *escarpena*; in Cataluña, *cap roig*, and in the Basque Country, *kabrarroka*. In this recipe, the scorpionfish's incredible flavor really shines through, while its appearance is cleverly disguised.

Pastel de cabracho
Red scorpionfish cake

INGREDIENTS (SERVES 4)

1lb 2oz scorpionfish, scaled

1 tablespoon butter

2 tablespoons dried natural
    bread crumbs

2 large tomatoes

3 tablespoons olive oil

pinch of salt

pinch of sugar

4 eggs

salt and white pepper, to taste

10oz phyllo pastry, cut into
    triangular pieces

2 tablespoons butter, melted

GARNISH

thin strands of leek, deep-fried

edible flower petals, from
    nasturtiums and marigolds
    (optional)

Put the fish in a saucepan, cover with water, and bring to a boil over a medium heat. Cook just long enough so that the fish flakes off the bones and skin easily. Set aside to cool.

Preheat the oven to 400°F. Grease a 2lb non stick loaf pan with butter and sprinkle bread crumbs over the sides.

Puree the tomatoes. Heat the olive oil in a skillet and cook the tomatoes with the salt and sugar over a low heat for 10 minutes. Allow to cool.

Beat the eggs until fluffy and pale, fold in the fish and tomato sauce, and season with salt and pepper. Pour into the prepared dish.

Sit the loaf pan in a deep roasting pan and pour in enough hot water to come three-quarters of the way up the sides. Then carefully put in the oven for 30 minutes. Remove from the oven, and set aside to cool. Turn the oven down to 350°F.

Brush the phyllo pastry triangles with butter and lay on a baking sheet. Bake in the oven for about 3 minutes until golden and crisp.

Turn the fish cake out of the loaf pan onto a cutting board, and cut into slices, about ¾ inch thick. Arrange 2 slices on each plate, accompanied by some phyllo pastry crisps. Garnish with the crisp leek and edible flower petals, if desired.

WINE TIPS

SPECIAL OCCASION: Organza, Señorío de San Vicente, Rioja (€€€)

SUNDAY LUNCH: Blanco Fernández de Piérola, Rioja Alavesa (€€)

EVERYDAY: Axpe, José Antonio Bilbao, Bizkaiko Txakolina (€)

Duck is now trendy in Spain. In addition to its tasty, succulent meat, the liver is used in many elegant recipes in the Basque Country. Here, the combination of cherries, almonds, and rose petals produces a fragrant dish, which bombards the senses with a plethora of aromas and colors.

Foie asado sobre cerezas con emulsión de almendras y sal de rosas

Roasted duck liver on cherries with rose-scented almond cream

INGREDIENTS (SERVES 4):

FOR THE ALMOND CREAM
2oz almond paste
3¹/2 cups blanched almonds, chopped
³/4 cup milk
1 garlic clove
Sherry wine vinegar
olive oil

FOR THE DUCK LIVER
1 fresh duck liver
8 large fresh juicy red cherries, pitted and halved
1 cup dried rose petals
1 teaspoon sea salt

GARNISH
sea salt flakes
1³/4oz dried rose petals
sprigs of fresh marjoram

Put the almond paste, almonds, milk, and garlic in a food processor, and blend to a cream. Add a little vinegar to adjust the sweetness and olive oil to correct the consistency. Pour into a bowl and keep in the refrigerator until needed.

Preheat the oven to 350°F. Put the duck liver under a hot broiler for 2 minutes, then finish cooking in the oven for another 2 or 3 minutes until cooked through.

Arrange 4 halves of cherry in the center of each plate. Put a quarter of the hot duck liver on top. Garnish with sea salt flakes, rose petals, and sprigs of fresh marjoram. Serve with the almond cream.

WINE TIPS
SPECIAL OCCASION: **Barón de Chirel, Marqués de Riscal, Rioja Alavesa (€€€)**
SUNDAY LUNCH: **Conde de Valdemar Crianza, Rioja Alavesa (€€)**
EVERYDAY: **Pérez Irazu Joven, Rioja Alaves (€)**

In the País Vasco, hake is one fish that is consumed all year round, in numerous guises. Basque-style hake is traditionally cooked in a casserole, but this recipe delivers a delicious plate of hake with a great deal more style and finesse.

Merluza a la vasca con guisantes de caserío y puntas de espárragos con yodo de perejil

Hake, Basque style, with green peas, asparagus tips, and parsley

INGREDIENTS (SERVES 4)

1lb 8oz hake fillet
1³/4 cups fresh peas, shelled
1/2 cup butter
16 white asparagus spears
salt, to taste

FOR THE STOCK

2lb 4oz hake bones and heads
1 onion, chopped
1 leek, chopped
2 tomatoes, chopped
1 carrot, chopped

FOR THE SAUCE

6 tablespoons olive oil
2 garlic cloves, sliced
1 onion, well chopped
3 tablespoons flour
1 cup fresh parsley, chopped
salt and white pepper

GARNISH

1 tablespoon olive oil
1 tablespoon chopped parsley

To make the stock, put all the ingredients in a large saucepan. Cover with water, bring to a boil, and cook over a medium heat for 30 minutes. Strain the stock through a sieve into a bowl and set aside.

For the sauce, heat the olive oil in a skillet over a medium heat. Add the garlic and onion, and sauté until just golden. Stir the flour into the olive oil with a wooden spoon and cook for 45 seconds. Then pour in about 2½ cups of the fish stock and cook, stirring continuously, until the sauce bubbles and thickens slightly. Stir in parsley and season with salt and pepper.

Cut the hake fillet into 4 pieces. Brush the hake with oil, place on a broiler rack and cook under a hot broiler for 6 minutes on each side.

Bring a saucepan of lightly-salted water to the boil, drop in the peas and blanch for about 5 minutes, or until tender. Drain off the hot water, then set aside.

Bring another saucepan of lightly salted water to a boil, add the butter, and drop in the asparagus. Blanch for about 3 minutes until just tender. Drain off the hot water, cut in half lengthwise and set aside.

For the garnish, mix the olive oil and parsley and allow to infuse for 15 minutes.

Place a piece of broiled hake on each plate and spoon a few fresh peas on top. Arrange some asparagus tips around the fish, and pour a little sauce onto each plate. Garnish with a drizzle of parsley oil.

WINE TIPS

SPECIAL OCCASION: **Erre Punto (R.) Blanco, Remirez de Ganuza, Rioja Alavesa (€€€)**
SUNDAY LUNCH: **Marqués de Riscal Blanco, Rueda (€€)**
EVERYDAY: **Xarmant, Arabako Txakolina (€)**

Fish and seafood soup is a mainstay of Spanish cuisine. Per head of population, Spain is the second-largest consumer of fish in the world. Each region has its own recipes, but those from the Basque Country are probably the best. To make a seafood soup requires fresh and varied ingredients, and enormous patience. The result is usually a magnificent feast, and well worth the time and effort involved.

Sopa de mariscos y pescado

Traditional fish and seafood soup

INGREDIENTS (SERVES 4)

8lb 12oz bones and heads from hake and anglerfish

6lb 8oz lobster, shrimp, and langoustine heads

4 tablespoons olive oil

1 carrot, diced

1 leek, finely chopped

1 large onion, finely chopped

2 garlic cloves, finely chopped

2 ripe tomatoes, skinned and chopped

4oz bread, sliced

1 cup tomato sauce

1/2 cup brandy

1 1/4 cups white wine

GARNISH

2 tablespoons olive oil

3 garlic cloves, chopped

7oz various fish flesh (hake, angler fish, grouper)

4 shrimp

4 langoustines

8 clams

1 cup brandy

1 tablespoon chopped parsley

To make a quantity of fish stock, put half the fish bones and heads in a large saucepan, cover with water, bring to a boil and simmer over a medium heat for 30 minutes, then strain.

Heat 2 tablespoons olive oil in a large saucepan and sauté the remaining fish bones and heads and the shellfish heads, in batches. Combine all the prepared vegetables, except the tomatoes, in a bowl and drizzle with 1 tablespoon olive oil; set aside.

To start making the soup, heat 1 tablespoon of olive oil in a large, clean saucepan. Add the tomatoes and simmer for 15 or 20 minutes. Add the sliced bread, sauté, and then add the tomato sauce.

Allow to cook for 20 minutes, then add the brandy. Once reduced by half, add the white wine. When the liquid has reduced by half again, add the prepared vegetables, and leave everything to cook together for 15 minutes.

After this time, add the fish stock and simmer over a low heat for 50 minutes. Allow the soup to cool a little before pouring into a food processor and blending until completely smooth.

Now make the garnish. In a skillet, heat the olive oil over a high heat, add the garlic and sauté briefly, without browning. Then add the fish pieces, shrimp, langoustines, and clams, and sauté for 5 minutes. Drench in brandy, heat, and flambé.

Ladle some soup into each bowl, and arrange a good selection of the sautéed fish and shellfish on top as a garnish. Finish with a sprinkling of chopped parsley.

WINE TIPS

SPECIAL OCCASION: **Remelluri Blanco, Rioja Alavesa (€€€)**
SUNDAY LUNCH: **Cosme Palacio Blanco, Palacio, Rioja Alavesa (€€)**
EVERYDAY: **Txakolina, Txomin Etxaniz, Getariako Txakolina (€)**

Wines of País Vasco

This far north, white grapes ripen more readily than red. This, coupled with the readily available seafood, has resulted in the local wines (all called Txakoli/Chacolí) being predominantly white. The main grape is the Hondarribi Zuri, which is not found anywhere else in the world, and the wines are light and very fresh, with crisp acidity and sometimes a residual hint of sparkle to tickle the tongue.

NB: the southern part of the province of Álava produces wines under the DOCa Rioja, and these are discussed in the chapter on La Rioja.

DO GETARIAKO TXAKOLINA/CHACOLÍ DE GUETARIA
The first of the Txakoli areas to be delimited, in 1990, it covers an area of land around the coastal towns of Getaria and Zarautz, inland as far as Aia in the province of Gipuzkoa (Guipúzcoa).

DO BIZKAIKO TXAKOLINA/CHACOLÍ DE VIZCAYA
A widely spread area from the coast, well inland and completely surrounding the city of Bilbao. Many plantations are very small indeed, including some tiny plots within the city itself.

DO ARABAKO TXAKOLINA/CHACOLÍ DE ÁLAVA
The smallest and most recent (2002) of the areas, in the province of Álava, mainly around the town of Amurrio. There are only three bodegas and one of them, Arabako Txakolina, is responsible for more than 90 percent of all production.

OTHER DRINKS
Along with its north-coast neighbors, the Basque Country has a thriving *sidra* (cider) industry, particularly in Gipuzkoa, which started making cider on a commercial scale in the 1930s. They describe it as "hard" or "natural" cider, and it's made with wild apples grown in the woodland orchards of the province. The cider-maker can choose from a number of varieties, including Geza, Miña, and Moko for bitterness; Manttoni, Txalaka, Urtebi txiki, and Urtebi haundi for acidity; and Mozolua and Patzoloa for sweetness. Every *sidreria* has a different formula, of course, but chemical additions are forbidden. The *sidra de Gipuzkoa* even has its own specially designed bottle. Although they recommend holding it at least 12 inches above the glass for pouring to aerate the cider, they don't demand the physical contortions favored by the *Asturianos*.

Main Bodegas
(listed in alphabetical order), PRODUCER NAME; town/village; web/E-mail address; best wines (r = red, w = white) A star (*) indicates particularly good quality.

DO GETARIAKO TXAKOLINA/CHACOLÍ DE GUETARIA
www.getariakotxakolina.com

TALAI-BERRI; Zarautz; www.talaiberri.com; Talai-Berri (w)

TXOMIN ETXANIZ; Getaria; www.txominetxaniz.com; Txomin Etxaniz (w)

DO BIZKAIKOTXAKOLINA/CHACOLÍ DE VIZCAYA
www.bizkaikotxakolina.org

ITURRIALDE; Mungia; www.gorkaizagirre.com; Aretxondo (w), Egia Enea (w)*

BEROJA; Muxica; www.bodegaberroja.com; Agirrebeko (w)

ITSASMENDI; Gernika; www.bodegasitsasmendi.com; Itsasmendi (w), Aihen (w)

DO ARABAKO TXAKOLINA/CHACOLÍ DE ÁLAVA
www.txakolidealava.com

ARABAKO TXAKOLINA; Amurrio; www.arabakotxakolina.com; Xarmant (w)

BELDIU; Llodio; www.beldiu.com; Beldiu (w)

Valencia is Spain's third city and biggest wine port; the export culture runs deep among the major bodegas, which supply a good deal of Europe's supermarket trade. Historically, the region is part of "greater Cataluña," and the local language, Valenciano, is a dialect of Catalan—road and direction signs are careful to spell it as València as well as in the Castilian style. The city, however, is extremely cosmopolitan, thanks to its seafaring and trading culture, and most European languages can be heard. The architect Santiago Calatrava was born here, and shot to fame as the designer of the Olympic stadium in Barcelona in 1992.

Valencia

In the 21st century, he returned home and helped to create the magnificent City of Arts and Sciences, which revitalized the central part of the city. The region consists of three provinces: Castelló de la Plana in the north, Valencia in the center, and Alicante to the south, all of them along the east coast.

LOCAL SPECIALTIES

Oranges are what most people think of when Valencia is mentioned; indeed, the Valencia oval is the most important variety in the world of orange cultivation. But it's not all citrus fruit: *kaki de la Ribera del Xúquer* is a variety of persimmon, mainly grown in Carlet and l'Alcudia, about 25 miles south of the city. *Nísperos de Callosa d'en Sarrià* are medlars grown about 12 miles inland from Calpe on the Alicante coast. *Uva de Mesa Embolsada Vinalopó* are table grapes ripened inside transparent bags to protect them from insects and fungal diseases in an area near the Murcian border with Alicante, about 25 miles west of Elche, which itself is famous for melons, and *cerezas de la montana de Alicante* are cherries grown in the highlands of northern Alicante and southern Valencia provinces.

One of Valencia's main crops is rice, with the biggest paddy fields in Europe, and exports to China, among other countries. *Paella* was first made, according to legend, in Dénia in Alicante. *Chufa de València* are tiger nuts (which are also turned into tiger-nut milk) just north of the city of Valencia; and the province of Castelló de la Plana is famous for its artichokes: *alcachofa de Benicarló* has been grown around the town for several centuries.

Elsewhere the region is as rich in local produce as the rest of Spain, with marks of quality for honey, olive oil, spicy pork products, including *longaniza* (flavored with chilies and/or spices) and *morcilleta* (black pudding, sometimes with onions and/or peppers). *Cordero Guirro* is a breed of sheep unique to the Valencia region.

In Valencia, there have always been numerous vegetable gardens, as well as chickens, rabbits, and rice paddies: it was only a matter of time before all these ingredients came together in a single dish, the *paella*, which is now a culinary icon in Spanish culture. There are many ways of assembling a *paella*, but the traditional version stays loyal to the local ingredients, plus saffron and a selection of seafood.

Paella Valenciana

Paella, Valencia-style

INGREDIENTS (SERVES 4)

2 tablespoons olive oil

1lb rabbit meat, cut into
small pieces

1lb 5oz chicken breast, cut into
small pieces

10oz fine green beans,
cut into 3/4 inch lengths

5oz white string beans, cut into
3/4 inch lengths

1 cup lima beans

4 oz tomatoes, skinned, seeded,
and finely chopped

2 cups short-grain rice

1 tablespoon paprika

pinch of saffron strands

3 1/2 cups water

salt and pepper, to taste

6oz clams, shells on

12 baby octopus

8 baby squid

GARNISH

sprigs of fresh dill

4 jumbo shrimp, cooked (optional)

Heat the olive oil in a *paellera* (paella pan) or a very large skillet, over a medium heat. When the oil is hot, add the rabbit and chicken, and sauté until golden brown.

Next add all the chopped beans. Continue to cook the mixture for an additional 8 minutes, before adding the tomatoes.

Stir until the mixture dries out a little, then add the rice, paprika, saffron, and water to the pan and mix well. Bring to a boil over a medium heat, season with salt and pepper, then add the clams, baby octopus, and squid. Reduce the heat and continue to cook, without stirring, for 16-18 minutes, until the rice is tender but not dry.

Spoon some *paella* into each bowl. Garnish with sprigs of fresh dill and a large cooked shrimp, if desired.

WINE TIPS

SPECIAL OCCASION: **Generación 1, Vicente Gandía Pla, Utiel-Requena (€€€)**
SUNDAY LUNCH: **Casa Don Ángel Bobal, Vere de Estenas, Utiel-Requena (€€)**
EVERYDAY: **Almuvedre, Telmo Rodríguez, Alicante (€)**

The taverns, *chiringuitos* (refreshment stands), and small bars along the Valencian coast are magnets for hungry bathers, attracted by the appetizing aroma of seafood grilling over hot charcoal. Shrimp from the Dénia area are especially famous for their sweet flavor and pinkness. Drizzling a little smoky-scented charcoal oil over this light broth is designed to evoke the magical smell of those open-air grills.

Gambas de Dénia al aceite de carbón

Dénia shrimp with charcoal oil

INGREDIENTS (SERVES 4)

2 tablespoons olive oil
1 garlic clove, chopped
1 teaspoon paprika
1 onion, chopped
1 carrot, chopped
1 leek, chopped
1 teaspoon cayenne pepper
2 sprigs of tarragon, chopped
2 sprigs of chervil, chopped
2oz shrimp shells
3 lobster heads
2lb 4oz shrimp
1 tablespoon Cognac
1/3 cup short-grain rice
16 raw jumbo shrimp
salt and pepper, to taste

FOR THE CHARCOAL OIL

2 cups rice bran
1 cup lapsang souchong China tea leaves
2 tablespoons olive oil
fresh herbs, to garnish (optional)

For the stock, heat the olive oil in a large stockpot over a low heat. Sauté the garlic until lightly golden, stir in the paprika, then tip in all the vegetables, and sweat until tender but not browned. Mix in the cayenne, tarragon, and chervil, and add the shrimp shells, lobster heads, and shrimp. Sauté over a medium heat until browned. Pour in the Cognac, heat briefly, then flambé.

Pour in the rice, cover with plenty of water, and bring to a boil over a medium heat. Then turn down the heat and simmer for 1 hour. Remove the stockpot from the heat, strain the stock through a sieve into a bowl, and allow to cool. Season to taste with salt and pepper, and set aside.

For the charcoal oil, toast the rice bran in the oven at 250°F, until totally blackened like "charcoal." Mix with the tea, which provides the smoky flavor, and blitz to a fine powder in a coffee grinder. Store the powder in a dry, airtight container to preserve the smoky aroma. Just before serving, mix 2 teaspoons of the charcoal powder into the olive oil.

Peel the jumbo shrimp, removing the tails but leaving the heads on. Rub with olive oil, sprinkle with a little salt and place under a hot broiler for about 2 minutes, turning once, until evenly pink all over.

Arrange 4 jumbo shrimp in the center of each shallow bowl, and pour in a little shellfish stock. Drizzle a few drops of the charcoal oil over the top. Garnish with fresh herbs, if desired.

WINE TIPS

SPECIAL OCCASION: **Verdeval Especial Roble, Vins del Comtat, Comunidad Valenciana (€€€)**
SUNDAY LUNCH: **Verderón, Casa del Pinar, Utiel Requena (€€)**
EVERYDAY: **Enrique Mendoza Chardonnay, Alicante (€)**

Langostinos from Vinarós hold a special place of honor among the produce of the Levante area. Up to 8 inches long, with a bright pink color, they are the colorful giants of the shrimp world. Their sweet, juicy flesh has always dazzled and beguiled great chefs. When combined with the juice of local oranges and rice, the langoustines more than live up to their reputation for being absolutely delicious.

Emulsión de erizo de mar con arroz de langostinos de Vinarós y sofrito de naranja

Sea urchins with langoustines, rice, and orange

INGREDIENTS (SERVES 4)

4 tablespoons olive oil

1 onion, finely chopped

1 leek, finely sliced

2 tomatoes, skinned, seeded, and chopped

7oz oranges

9oz anglerfish, cut into small pieces

roe of 2 sea urchins, sliced (remove the spines, wash the shells and save for later) plus 6 more spineless washed sea urchin shells

1½ cups short-grain rice

4 cups fish stock

8 raw langoustines, shelled

8 small clams, shells on

salt and pepper, to taste

handful of fresh mint leaves, finely chopped, to garnish

Heat 2 tablespoons of the olive oil in a large saucepan, and sauté the onion and leek until golden. Then add the tomatoes and cook for 4 minutes.

Squeeze the juice from the oranges and add to the saucepan with the fish. Cook for 2 minutes, then stir in the sea urchin roe until covered with orange juice.

Tip the rice and fish stock into the saucepan, and simmer over a medium heat for 10 minutes. Then mix in the langoustines and clams, and cook for an additional 3 minutes. Stir gently with a wooden spoon, mix in the remaining olive oil, season with salt and pepper, and set aside to rest.

Place 2 spineless sea urchin shells on each plate. Fill all the shells with rice and fish, and serve with 2 langoustines and 2 clams per portion. Garnish with a light sprinkling of fresh mint.

WINE TIPS

SPECIAL OCCASION: **Casta Divi Monte Diva, Gutiérrez de la Vega, Alicante (€€€)**

SUNDAY LUNCH: **Las Tres, Chozas Carrascal, Utiel-Requena (€€)**

EVERYDAY: **Murviedro Blanco, Valencia (€)**

Spain has the largest area of date palms under cultivation in Europe. Introduced by the Berbers of the Sahara, their splendid legacy is best seen in the magnificent *Palmeral de Elche*, where 200,000 date palms grow in a series of orchards and produce 8,000 tons of dates a year. The sweet, luscious, golden fruit harmonizes perfectly with the nuts and chocolate in this recipe.

Pastel de guianduja con chocolate y dátiles dulces de Elche en texturas frías y calientes

Hot and cold hazelnut praline cake with chocolate and Elche dates

INGREDIENTS (SERVES 4)

FOR THE *GUIANDUJA*
1/3 cup superfine sugar
1 cup toasted hazelnuts, chopped
6oz milk chocolate

FOR THE CHOCOLATE MOUSSE
3/4 cup whipping cream
6oz semisweet chocolate
1/2 cup heavy cream
pinch of Chinese five spice powder

FOR THE *GUIANDUJA* MOUSSE
3/4 cup heavy cream
1 sheet of leaf gelatin, soaked
9oz *guianduja* (see above)
11/2 cups whipping cream
4 dates, thinly sliced

FOR THE CHOCOLATE GLAZE
1/2 cup water
5 tablespoons liquid glucose
4 sheets of leaf gelatin, soaked
7oz bittersweet chocolate

For the *guianduja*, put the sugar and hazelnuts in a small heavy saucepan over a medium heat until the sugar turns golden brown. Remove from the heat and stir to coat the hazelnuts. Line a baking sheet with paper parchment, and carefully pour the hot nutty caramel onto the sheet. Spread out thinly, and allow to cool until brittle. Smash 9oz of the hazelnut praline into a rough mixture (*not* a powder) in a food processor. Set the rest of the sheet aside. Break the chocolate into a bowl, and melt over a saucepan of simmering water. Stir in the crushed praline, and set aside.

For the chocolate mousse, pour the whipping cream into a saucepan and bring to a boil. Break the semisweet chocolate into a bowl and pour in the hot cream. Stir well until the chocolate has melted. When the chocolate cream has cooled, but is still slightly warm, stir in the heavy cream and five spice powder. Half fill four 1½oz ingot molds (mini individual loaf tins would be suitable) with the spicy chocolate cream, and set aside to cool, before putting in the refrigerator to set.

For the *guianduja* mousse, bring the cream to a boil in a saucepan, and stir in the gelatin until dissolved. Stir into the *guianduja* (see above) and mix well. When the mixture has cooled slightly, stir in the whipping cream, and pour into the half-filled molds, and top with the dates. Allow to cool, before putting in the refrigerator to set.

For the chocolate glaze, bring the water and glucose to a boil in a small saucepan, and remove from the heat. Stir in the gelatin until dissolved. Break the chocolate into a bowl, then pour the hot sweet water over the chocolate.

Lay 4 pieces of the remaining *guianduja* on a wire cake-cooling rack. Turn out the chilled mousses and place on top of the *guianduja*. Top with chocolate glaze.

WINE TIPS

SPECIAL OCCASION: **Dolç de Mendoza, Alicante (€€€)**
SUNDAY LUNCH: **Casta Diva Miel, Gutiérrez de la Vega, Alicante (€€)**
EVERYDAY: **Fusta Nova, Vicente Gandía Pla, Valencia (€)**

Wines of Valencia

Because of the region's focus on exports, particularly of supermarket wines, it's hard to put a style on the wines of Valencia. The main red grapes are the Monastrell and the Bobal, but with increasing amounts of Tempranillo, Cabernet Sauvignon, *et al*; the main white is the Merseguera, which turns out pleasant but unexceptional everyday wines. The terrain ranges from sea level to about 2,0450 feet, so there's a range of microclimates for those bodegas prepared to do more than churn out millions of bottles for the mass market. Bobal, formerly seen only as a grape for bulk wines, is turning out to be a very promising grape in the right hands, and several of the more forward-looking bodegas have been experimenting with low-yielding older vines with some considerable success.

Monastrell has been rehabilitated here, and is now seen as a real contender for quality wines rather than just a base for blending. Most reds from Alicante are based on this, with Tempranillo and Bobal (especially in Utiel-Requena) a close second. There is some white wine made from Chardonnay, and a few bodegas are working with Merlot and Syrah. The Valencia DO is also a center for sweet wines made from Malvasía, Moscatel, and Pedro Ximénez, usually singly but occasionally in blends. These are some of the best-value sweet wines from Spain

DO ALICANTE
The southernmost DO of the region, with two subzones: one on the coast north of Calpe, the other around and west of Alicante city. They grow Monastrell, Garnacha, and Bobal for reds, Merseguera and Moscatel for whites.

DO UTIEL-REQUENA
The furthest inland, next door to the Manchuela DO (Murcia). Bobal is the chief grape, but Tempranillo is second and there is work with Cabernet Sauvignon and Syrah. Vineyards range from 1,969 to 2,953 feet so there is potential here for excellent wines, yet to be fully realized.

DO VALENCIA
This is divided into three subzones, with vineyards from 656 to 2,050 feet growing mainly Monastrell and Garnacha for reds and Merseguera for whites. The "Moscatel de Valencia" area for sweet wines is immediately west of the city itself.

OTHER WINES
Valencia has had a number of country-wine areas, including Benniarés and Lliber-Javea (both in Alicante), many of which are now unofficial. The only two currently registered are these:

VdlT Castelló In Castelló de la Plana, this area was created in 2001 and grows Bobal, Garnacha, Tempranillo, and others for reds, and Chardonnay, Malvasia, and others for whites. The wines are not well known outside the area

VdlT Terrerazo This is, perhaps, an example of a high-profile bodega winning its own little VdlT classification (*see* Guelbenzu, in Navarra). The bodega below has resolutely refused to join the Utiel-Requena DO, in spite of being within the area and working with the Bobal grape.

Other bodegas have chosen not to belong to any of the official wine areas. The most enduring is in Alicante.

OTHER DRINKS

With a well-developed wine-based culture, it was inevitable that the Valencia region should have a wide range of alcoholic drinks. These include *anis paloma de monrote del Cid*, an anise spirit made about 12 miles west of Alicante; *aperitivo café de Alcoy* is an infused coffee liqueur made in Alcot, about 37 miles north of Alicante; *cantueso Alicantino* is a unique, thyme-based liqueur, made in the province of Alicante and aged in oak; and *herbero de la Sierra de Mariola* is a herbal infusion from the Sierra de Mariola National Park in Alicante.

By far the most widespread wine-based drink, however, is *fondillón*, made mainly around Monóvar, about 25 miles west of the city of Alicante. Overripe Monastrell grapes (which may also be sun-dried) are fermented and may achieve up to 16 percent alcohol by volume, after which they are mixed with older wines and allowed to mature. Good *fondillón* has a warm, nutty character, a hint of acidity, and a generous, silky finish, and is much in demand as an after-dinner drink.

Main Bodegas

(listed in alphabetical order), PRODUCER NAME; town/village; web/E-mail address; best wines (r = red, w = white) A star (*) indicates particularly good quality.

DO ALICANTE
www.crdo-alicante.org

ENRIQUE MENDOZA; Alfaz del Pi; www.bodegasmendoza.com; Enrique Mendoza (r)*; Dolç de Mendoza (sweet r)*

GUTIÉRREZ DE LA VEGA; Parcent; www.castadiva.es; Casta Diva (sweet w)*

TELMO RODRÍGUEZ; Logroño; cia@fer.es; El Sequé (r)*

DO UTIEL-REQUENA
www.utielrequena.org

CASA DEL PINAR; Venta del Moro; www.casadelpinar.com; Casa del Pinar (r)*

VICENTE GANDÍA; Chiva; www.gandiawines.com; Hoya de Cadenas (r); Generación 1 (r)*

DO VALENCIA
www.vinovalencia.org

BELDA; Fontanars dels Alforins; www.vinsbjb.com; Daniel Belda (r)

MURVIEDRO; Requna; www.murviedro.es; Estrella (sweet w); Los Monteros (r)

VdlT TERRERAZO

MUSTIGUILLO; Las Cuevas de Utiel; mustiguillo@inicia.es; Finca Terrerazo (r); Quincha Corral (r)*

VINS DEL COMTAT; Cocentaina; www.vinsdelcomtat.com; Montcabrer (r); Penya Cadiella Selecció (r)*

Recommended restaurants

(City names within province listings in italics)

The very best restaurants are annotated below with a star.

ANDALUCÍA

Almería City: La Gruta.

Cádiz City: El Faro. **Province:** *Arcos de la Frontera:* El Convento; *Los Barrios:* El Copo; *Jerez de la Frontera:* La Mesa Redonda; *Puerto de Santa María:* El Faro del Puerto; *Sanlúcar de Barrameda:* Bigote, El Veranillo.

Córdoba City: Almudaína, El Caballo Rojo, Pic-Nic.

Granada City: Chikito, Los Santanderinos. **Province:** *Cenes de la Vega:* Ruta del Veleta.

Huelva City: Farqueo, Las Meigas. **Province:** *Aracena:* José Vicente; *Isla Cristina:* Casa Rufino; *Punta Umbría:* El Paraíso.

Jaén City: Casa Antonio. **Province:** *Baeza:* Juanito; *Cazorla:* La Sarga.

Málaga City: Adolfo, Café de Paris. **Province:** *Churriana:* La Cónsula (a highly regarded catering college); *Estepona:* La Alcaría de Ramos; *Fuengirola:* El Higuerón; *Marbella:* La Hacienda, El Lago, Ruperto de Nola; *Santiago El Palo:* Mamé; **Sevilla City:** Egaña Oriza, Taberna de Alabardero.

Province: *Sanlúcar la Mayor:* La Alquería.

ARAGÓN

Huesca City: Lillas Pastia, Las Torres, Venta del Sotón.

Province: *Barbastro:* Flor; *Hecho:* Gaby-Casa Blasquico; *Jaca:* La Cocina Aragonesa, Lilium; *Aínsa:* Bodegas del Sobrabre, Bodegón de Mallacan, Callizo; *Panticosa:* Lago.

Teruel City: La Menta, La Tierreta. **Province:** *Tramacastilla:* El Batán; *Cantavieja:* Buj.

Zaragoza City: El Cachirulo, Gayarre, Goyesco, La Ontina, Txalupa. **Province:** *Cariñena:* La Rebótica; *Villanueva de Gallego:* Sella-La Val d'Onsella.

ASTURIAS

Oviedo: L'Alezna, Casa Conrado, Del Arco, Casa Fermin.

Gijón: Casa Victor, Paladares, Casa Zabala. **Province:** *Arriondas:* El Corral del Indianu; *Avilés:* Real Balneario; *Mareo:* La Solana; *Prendes:* Casa Gerardo; *La Salgar:* Casa Marcial.

THE BALEARIC ISLANDS

Palma de Mallorca: El Jardin de Son Vida, Koldo Royo, Plat d'Or, Porto Pí, Read's. **Province:** *Andratx:* Miramar; *Bunyola:* Ses Porxeres; *Capdepera:* Ses Rotges; *Deià:* El Olivo, Ca'n Ouet; *Pollença:* Cavall Bernat; *Portals Nous:* Tristán; *Sóller:* Béns d'Avall.

CANARY ISLANDS

Lanzarote: *Yaiza:* La Era. **Tenerife:** *Playa de las Américas:* Bahía del Duque, El Patio; *Puerto de la Cruz:* Botánico; *Santa Cruz de Tenerife:* Mencey.

CANTABRIA

Santander: La Cúpula del Rhin, El Puntal, El Serbal.

Province: *Escalante:* San Román de Escalante; *Ramales de la Victoria:* Río Asón; *Torrelavega:* Los Avellanos; *Villaverde de Pontones:* Cenador de Amós.

CASTILLA Y LEÓN

Ávila province: *Hoyos del Espino:* El Milano Real.

Burgos city: El Ángel, Landa Palace.

León city: Vivaldi. **Province:** *Astorga:* La Peseta.

Palencia city: Casa Lucio. **Province:** *Carrión de los Condes:* Estrella del Bajo Carrión.

Salamanca city: Chez Victor, Victor Gutiérrez.

Segovia city: La Cocina de Segovia, Mesón de Cándido.

Province: *Cañicosa:* Codex Calixtinus.

Soria city: Rincón de San Juan.

Zamora city: El Rincón de Antonio, Paris. **Province:** *Benavente:* El Ermitano.

CASTILLA LA MANCHA

Albacete city: Nuestro Bar, Casa Paco. **Province:** *Almansa:* Mesón de Pincelín.

Ciudad Real city: Miami Park. **Province:** *Almagro:* El Corregidor.

Cuenca province: *Las Pedroñeras:* Las Rejas; *Villalba de la Sierra:* Mesón Nelia.

Guadalajara province: *Marchamalo:* La Llaves; *Sigüenza:* Calle Mayor.

Toledo city: La Alacena. **Province:** *Illescas:* El Bohío.